LABORATORY SCHOOLS

An Educational Resource

National Association of
Laboratory Schools

Curriculum Research & Development Group
University of Hawaii
Honolulu
1991

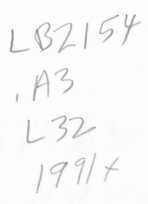
Published by
the Curriculum Research & Development Group
University of Hawaii
1776 University Avenue
Honolulu, Hawaii 96822

ISBN 0–937049–65–4

Publication assistance by Independent Resources, Honolulu

Printed by Thomson-Shore, Inc.

Printed in the United States of America

To
the administrators,
teachers,
and
children
of laboratory schools

The country needs . . . bold, persistent
experimentation.
It is common sense to take a method and try it:
If it fails, admit it frankly and try another.

—Franklin Delano Roosevelt

Contents

Acknowledgments

EVENTS DURING THE LAST FEW DECADES have altered the course of laboratory schools across the nation. For that reason the directors of the National Association of Laboratory Schools (NALS) decided eight years ago that the time had come to publish a book updating the record and reflecting on the changes—no small task! Members of the NALS board surveyed the schools and sifted data. School directors and staff members assembled historical records, contemplated their own experience, and articulated their ideas in the essays assembled in this volume. Without them we would have no book.

Crayton L. Buck, director of the College Learning Laboratory at Buffalo State College, and Loretta Krause, principal of the University of Hawaii Laboratory School, co-chaired the publication committee. They solicited the essays, nudged their authors, and kept the project on track. The executive director of NALS, John R. Johnson, administrator of the University School at Indiana University of Pennsylvania, served as nerve center and troubleshooter.

The materials were assembled and edited in Hawaii at the Curriculum Research & Development Group (CRDG), of which the University Laboratory School is a part. Arthur R. King, Jr., the director of CRDG, massaged the manuscripts for coherence within the plan for the volume, with help from Ralph Williams, who also put the essays on the word processor. Edith K. Kleinjans, CRDG's house editor, then edited the revised manuscript. Kathleen Berg tracked down vagrant references and tied up other loose ends.

Photos came from collectors at the campus schools of Ball State University, Buffalo State College, Carnegie Mellon University, Eastern Washington University, Florida Atlantic University, Eastern Oregon State College, Hunter College, Indiana University of Pennsylvania, Keene College, and the University of Hawaii. Henry Bennett of Independent Resources handled design, production, and printing of the book.

An extra measure of gratitude goes to three friends of the University of Hawaii Laboratory School for their generosity in helping to underwrite the costs of this book. They are Takayoshi Mizushima of Tokyo, president of the Cultural Foundation on Promoting the National Costume of Japan; Masanori Sugo, principal of the Nishinippon Junior College High School in Yame city; and Kazumasa Okuda, director of the Sohseikan High School in Isahaya city. Mr. Mizushima assists the lab school in its kimono art project. The two schools are "sister schools" of the lab school.

Loretta Krause

Foreword

IT HAS BEEN TWENTY YEARS since C. Robert Blackmon of the University of Southwestern Louisiana assembled *Laboratory Schools, U.S.A.—Studies and Readings*. That volume carried sixteen articles about campus laboratory schools. Among the articles, some treated the schools' search for identity, their status, and their roles in educational research, curriculum development, and the education of teachers. Other articles looked at the past, speculated about the future, and profiled schools that performed oustanding work or departed from the pattern of sponsorship by a college or university.

At that time laboratory schools were under pressure to prove their value to the profession. With a slow job market for teachers, the need for sites for observation, demonstration, participation, and practice teaching had slackened. Research and experimentation were being pushed as promising roles for laboratory schools.

Some states were reviewing their campus schools to determine whether they were worth maintaining. By the mid-seventies, the number of such schools had declined to 166 from over 200 in 1964. By 1982 the number was down to 123.

In the interim from 1970 to 1990 a good many educators—Irving G. Hendrick, Francis S. Chase, John I. Goodlad, William Van Til, and Arthur R. King, Jr., among them—have written about the dilemmas of laboratory schools and advised concentration on experimentation, research and development, or other emerging areas of service. But they have also recognized that without resources the schools could do little. As William Van Til put it, the schools are "exhorted to make bricks yet supplied insufficient straw" (1987, 24).

This volume, prepared by the National Association of Laboratory Schools (NALS), tells what the schools have done about the dearth of straw—and how some have managed to make bricks despite the shortage.

The first chapter, "Laboratory Schools in Times of Change," reviews the responses of campus schools to changes from the time they were adjuncts to training academies, through the mid-century decades of social change, to recent decades of new demands and new challenges. It was written by two administrators, Crayton L. Buck of the College Learning Laboratory at Buffalo State College and Kenneth E. Miller of the Burris Laboratory School at Ball State University.

Chapter 2, "Functions of Laboratory Schools," surveys today's lab schools, showing which of the traditional roles they still fulfill, what newer ones they have taken on, and how they rank each of eight major functions. This chapter was written by Buck and four other lab school people: Robert Hymer, Jacksonville State University of Alabama; Gene McDonald, formerly of Southeastern Louisiana University; Jackson J. Martin, Eastern Washington State University; and Theodore S. Rodgers, University of Hawaii.

"Strategic Planning for Laboratory Schools: Concepts, Models, and Cases," Chapter 3, reports how seven schools have responded to changes and challenges. Ross A. Nielsen draws a "blueprint for laboratory school success" from his many years at Price Laboratory School, University of Northern Iowa. Lynn McCarthy and Albert Bertani of the National College of Education in Evanston, Illinois, offer a step-by-step guide for a self-study as a prerequisite to setting new directions. Then Charles V. Branch, of Metropolitan State College in Denver, recounts how the college and the public school system joined forces to convert a public elementary school into a cooperative laboratory school called Greenlee/Metro Laboratory School. Adrianne Bank explains how and why the elementary school of the University of California at Los Angeles became a "center of inquiry" into three areas of educational need. Buck describes how the College Learning Laboratory in Buffalo came to be a cooperative enterprise of State University College and the Buffalo school system, focusing on pre-service education of teachers. Ann Baldwin Taylor, head of the Children's School at Carnegie Mellon University, tells how her school serves dual roles as a research site for studies of child development and as a field experience site for students who plan to teach preschoolers. Finally, Arthur R. King, Jr., director of the Curriculum Research & Development

Group at the University of Hawaii, relates how the university's laboratory school switched its mission from assisting in teacher preparation to designing, developing, and disseminating curricula.

Chapter 4 compares the features and operations of laboratory schools in the United States and attached schools in Japan. Its authors are King of the University of Hawaii and Yasushi Mizoue of Hiroshima University.

In Chapter 5, "Governance and Financing of Laboratory Schools," Buck and Martin report on how schools share governance with their sponsoring institutions and where they get their financial support.

Chapter 6 showcases thirty-two lab schools that responded to an invitation to send descriptive sketches for inclusion in this volume. The schools are listed alphabetically by state.

"Campus Schools in the United States to 1965," Chapter 7, looks back to the early days. It consists of excerpts from a book in which the late Harry Hutton, of Pennsylvania State University, chronicled the evolution of these schools from the era of training schools and normal schools to the time when state teachers colleges became universities with colleges of education. Hutton's theme is the schools' slowness to respond to the imperative to experiment, research, and innovate—a theme that recurs in nearly every study of laboratory schools.

In the final chapter, eight lab school people pool their speculations about the future, posing answers to questions about niches for the schools, their relation to universities and school systems, and the conditions that lead to success or failure. The authors are Buck, King, and six others: Mina Bayne of the University of Wyoming, Roy Creek of the University of Pittsburgh, Judith Hechtman and John R. Johnson of Indiana University of Pennsylvania, Bart Tosto of Buffalo State College, and Gregory R. Ulm of Indiana State University. They predict that the innovative and competent among university-based schools will succeed to the degree that they respond creatively to the nationwide demand for educational improvement.

1

Laboratory Schools
in Times of Change

Crayton L. Buck and Kenneth E. Miller

SPECIAL-PURPOSE LABORATORY SCHOOLS, at first called "model schools" or "training schools," have been an important part of the American system for preparing teachers since the mid-1880s. Most are on the campuses of their sponsoring institutions and are often called "campus schools" or "campus laboratory schools." Over a hundred such schools now serve as sites for teacher training, research, and related functions for elementary and secondary schools. About a hundred others serve similar functions for preschools. Although these resources are substantial, such schools fulfill only a small fraction of the need. By far the greater proportion of clinical service to teacher education is supplied by regular public schools.

Education professionals and some members of the general community are now debating the proper environments for clinical practicums for teachers. Some argue for "typical" regular schools; the Holmes Group of major universities advocates the founding of "professional development schools"; people in the laboratory school tradition represented in this book believe that schools maintained by universities for the purposes of university-based programs are needed to provide the quality of services not available through other means.

Laboratory schools provided most clinical training in teacher-training institutions (normal schools and training academies and colleges) until the 1920s. Then they entered a period of change. During the 1930s, 1940s, and 1950s many of them were closed; others continued their traditional functions with limited support; some responded creatively to the demands for change, modifying their programs to emphasize research, curriculum development, in-service education, or service to special populations such as the handicapped or the gifted.

The background to these changes informs the current debate on the proper content and placement of clinical services. It also speaks to the general problem of how a once universally accepted organization, the laboratory school, was forced to adjust to a changing society, to a changing set of functions, and to changes in sponsoring institutions—the universities and colleges that prepare teachers, conduct research on education, and provide other services. The background also illuminates the complex nature of competition for recognition, resources, and respectability by teacher education programs.

LABORATORY SCHOOLS AS SITES FOR CLINICAL PRACTICE

During the nineteenth century, teacher training was carried out in a variety of normal schools and academies. Most such institutions were maintained by public school systems; some were operated by private schools with a sideline in preparing teachers. Few institutions preparing elementary school teachers had a base in higher education. High school teachers were more likely to be products of colleges and universities.

Fritz (1985) cites an example of the early standing of campus schools in the Normal School Act of 1857 passed by the Pennsylvania Legislature:

> Before designation as an official state normal school, each had to provide a ten-acre campus, housing for three hundred students, an auditorium capable of seating a thousand persons, rooms for libraries, a minimum of six faculty members, and a *model school of one hundred students*. [Italics added.]

The model training school was a necessity. Regular public schools were typically staffed by young teachers with limited academic and professional training. In the model school, the professor of pedagogy gave direction, shape, and supervision to the teacher-training process.

As the normal school movement spread rapidly across the country during the late 1800s and early 1900s, laboratory schools proliferated. At most, 70 percent of normal schools ever maintained their own model schools. But over time many teacher education institutions closed, and their campus schools closed with them. Most of the institutions that ceased to operate were ones associated with city and county school systems. By the turn of the century the responsibility for preparing teachers, particularly at the elementary level, had been transferred to teachers colleges, a new and rapidly growing segment of higher education.

The standing of campus schools was still strong in 1926 when the American Association of Teachers Colleges (A.A.T.C.) adopted Standard VII A. It mandated the following:

> Each teachers college shall maintain a training school under its own control as a part of its organization for the purposes of observation, demonstration and supervised teaching on the part of students. The use of an urban or rural school system, under sufficient control and supervision of the college to permit carrying out the educational policy of the college to a sufficient degree for the conduct of effective student teaching, will satisfy the requirement. (A.A.T.C. 1926)

Note that although a campus school was recommended, use of a public school as an alternative was accepted if there was a certain amount of college control. Compulsory education and the growing numbers of children in a rapidly growing nation had brought a demand for many more teachers. When some laboratory schools proved too small to accommodate the growing number of teachers in training, teachers colleges had to limit the numbers of students permitted to observe and practice there—or at least organize them so they didn't get in one another's way. Teachers colleges also had to find ways to accommodate the overflow of teacher trainees in public schools.

The practice of using multiple sites became so extensive that A.A.T.C. revised its standards to address the issue. In 1948 it changed Standard VII A, acknowledging that the practice of conducting most student teaching in laboratory schools was no longer feasible. Although the revised standard included campus schools, it clearly indicated that practice teaching in equivalent, accessible off-campus schools was not only permissible but desirable (Flowers 1948). Perhaps this was a case where standards were set by necessity.

THE OPTION OF PUBLIC SCHOOLS AS SITES FOR CLINICAL PRACTICE

Public school districts have long provided a variety of clinical teaching experiences. Most laboratory schools, in fact, began in local school districts, then were later institutionalized on college campuses in the national effort to upgrade teacher preparation.

When teachers colleges first turned to local public schools as sites for clinical practice, they found many participating teachers inept as clinical practitioners because they were short on theoretical knowledge and lacking in expertise as critics. And though public schools seemed to be natural settings for training, educators lamented their loss of control over training personnel. B. Othanel Smith (1980, 22) summarized the shortcomings of arrangements with public schools:

> From the beginning the use of public schools as a training facility rested on an uneasy partnership. Use of the schools was informally arranged. Neither the university nor the college of pedagogy negotiated contracts for the services of the schools. In moving its trainees to the schools, the college gained a natural setting for its training function, but lost control of the training personnel. The critic or supervising teachers were typically recommended, if not selected, by the principal, although the college sometimes exercised veto power. They were poorly paid, typically by small stipends or student waivers, and as critic teachers untrained; nor did the college provide training for them. Even today, only a few colleges provide a modicum

of training. Furthermore, the services of supervising teachers were over and beyond their normal teaching loads, overtaxing their energies and rendering them less effective as critics. Against all this was the claim that the teacher and the school profited from the growth of teachers who served as supervisors, a dubious claim at best.

But the major drawback, wrote Smith (1980, 12), was that using public schools as training sites left clinical work "largely under the control of and carried on by . . . personnel [who were] unprepared to train teachers."

With changes in public schooling during the intervening years have come changes in college-to-school arrangements. Now teachers themselves choose their roles in demonstration or supervision, and the arrangements may even be governed by union contract. As public demands for accountability and achievement have mounted, administrators and teachers have become more alert to the possibility of public displeasure with using schools for purposes other than teaching children. Keislar (1980, 29–30) addresses this point:

Recently, however, some investigators are finding greater resistance on the part of public schools in meeting requests for research. . . . Furthermore, school systems are becoming increasingly reluctant to engage in any activity which is out of the ordinary because of the possibility of legal action. Finally, administrative demands on both teacher and pupils leave less time for regular instruction.

Some colleges and universities, in their efforts to secure satisfactory field sites, have developed collaborative agreements that are binding on both parties. But they have found that differences in organization, attitudes, expectations, and needs pose problems. Rasmussen (1969) observed that even when school administrators were interested in having their schools used for observation, it was extraordinarily difficult for them to handle large numbers of student observers who needed to be in specific classrooms at specific times to observe specially planned and taught lessons structured to correlate with university methods, psychology, and curriculum classes.

IMPACT ON LABORATORY SCHOOLS OF THE CONVERSION OF
NORMAL SCHOOLS AND TEACHERS COLLEGES INTO
MULTIPURPOSE UNIVERSITIES

Even as the normal schools were modifying their programs, extending
the training periods, increasing specialization of teaching emphases,
and establishing new programs, seeds of change were being planted.
Critics and academicians began suggesting that the training of teachers
should be the responsibility of those with mastery of subject matter.
Normal schools responded by creating separate departments that set
the stage for the evolution to degree-granting teachers colleges and
then to multipurpose liberal arts institutions.

As normal schools lengthened their teacher-training programs,
they added course work to expand the knowledge base for teachers—a
natural response to the needs of a society setting priority on education
as a means for advancement. The numbers of faculty with expertise in
academic subjects grew in proportion to the curricular space allocated
to academic subjects. This remolding of the faculties diluted commitment to the single purpose of training teachers. People with competence in liberal arts subjects brought an orientation to the advancement of their subject area rather than to the advancement of teaching.

The accelerated movement to full degree-granting institutions,
first called teachers colleges, was abetted by the social conditions of
the Depression and World War II. During the Depression, resources
were severely constrained. With opportunities for employment limited
and funds for a college education hard to find, many young people
looked to teaching as an avenue to upward mobility. Normal schools
offered low-cost education within the means of many families. Many
normal school graduates achieved success in fields unrelated to teaching. Normal schools, many of which were struggling for survival at the
time, welcomed students who had no intention of becoming teachers.
College faculty members whose commitment to teacher training was
not strong became the dominant force in governance, controlling the
mechanisms that set goals and objectives for their institutions. They
were in a position to proselytize and gain commitment to expanded
functions, which eventually became reality.

The shift in faculty orientation heightened differences of opinion about the knowledge needed by teachers. It also brought about a more complex organization. The new departments that emerged to offer additional subjects did not necessarily work closely with teacher educators. In fact, they competed for resources and disagreed over the nature of teacher training as it related to theory and practice. Some of them showed disdain for the pedagogical emphasis in training, believing that professional courses lacked both rigor and a body of substantive knowledge, making them less worthy than the liberal arts. This persistent mind-set shifted the allocation of resources, ultimately affecting the fate of laboratory schools. Blackmon (1975) wrote that when teachers colleges metamorphosed into universities, the resulting faculties were quite removed from teacher education as a major interest, and when increasing enrollments produced fierce competition for dollars and space, these mainly arts-and-sciences-oriented faculties were willing to phase out the laboratory school. The teacher educators were outvoted.

With the transformation of normal schools into multipurpose institutions, faculties began abandoning pedagogy and the important relationship between liberal knowledge, pedagogy, and curriculum. Normal school faculties had shared the commitment to preparing teachers, devoting all their human and financial resources to this paramount purpose. But with faculties perceiving their roles in the liberal arts tradition, support for teacher education declined.

These changes, made in response to powerful societal forces, probably could not have been averted. But the responses of laboratory schools were often inappropriate.

IMPACT OF INTERNAL UNIVERSITY FORCES ON LABORATORY SCHOOLS

Colleges and universities are subject to internal pressures from their own governance systems and to external pressures from outside agencies.

Higher education, with its traditions of faculty consultation, collegiality, and control over the curriculum, provides a rich milieu for governance systems to operate. In any college or university, the advancement of a department's interests depends on how well it can manipulate the system. A department may form alliances to further its interests, but such links do not necessarily become permanent bonds. In the scramble for survival, competition for resources—financial, human, and physical—becomes formidable. Schools of education have had to compete not only with programs in the liberal arts and the professions but also with newer professional programs such as business, criminal justice, social work, and computer management.

The laboratory school, once integral to teacher education programs, has become just another department competing for resources. With professional education declining in university governance, laboratory schools have had few strong allies within their own institutions.

When large enrollments in the early 1960s forced colleges and universities to redefine priorities and programs and to cope with limited space and fiscal constraints, laboratory schools were caught in the crunch. Lack of space and money, not inability to perform useful functions, were the reasons given for closing many of them. Howd and Browne wrote in the report of their 1969 survey that between 1964 and 1969

> sixty-five schools were reported reduced in scope or in the process of closing. . . . Financial rather than educational need appeared to be the deciding factor in most decisions to close that were reported. Cost of operation and shortage of campus space caused by growing enrollments were the most frequently stated reasons. (Howd and Browne 1970, 5, 6)

IMPACT OF EXTERNAL FORCES ON LABORATORY SCHOOLS

While internal university forces were pressing on laboratory schools, the schools have also had to respond to outside pressures and accommodate to external decisions. Of the situation by 1972 McGeoch wrote that although

> the campus laboratory school was established in response to a clear need, . . . it continued and took on additional functions as

education beliefs and programs of teacher training changed and expanded. Within recent years, however, the processes of adaptation and accommodation have become inadequate. The campus school now finds itself confronted with the possibility of becoming . . . extinct. (McGeoch 1972, 8)

When laboratory schools accommodated unwisely, failure almost always followed. Unable to fulfill their role well, laboratory schools lost their exemplary character, and survival itself became an issue.

Pressures were exerted variously from higher education coordinating bodies, state education departments, legislatures, teachers' associations and unions, and local school districts. These groups had their own agendas and their own perceptions of the place of schools in society. Societal pressures also impacted laboratory schools. Blackmon (1975) mentions an egalitarian movement, desegregation, and a new emphasis on urban education for disadvantaged children; sputnik and the resulting priority given to mathematics and science; and the increasing number of innovations occurring outside the laboratory school, particularly federally funded curriculum development and educational technology.

Those in decision-making roles faced an array of problems and issues requiring resolution. When resources ran short, they had to generate alternatives. The laboratory school became a visible, appetizing target on many campuses. It had buildings easily converted to other uses. Its faculty members could be absorbed into other departments or retrenched. Its functions could be accomplished in public school districts, and the financial savings could advance new programs or strengthen existing ones.

Furthermore, because laboratory schools were perceived as elitist, no one worried that their students would be deprived of an education; they could go elsewhere. It is no surprise then that those who had to make decisions about funding laboratory schools suggested that they could be excised without harming the larger institutions.

Laboratory school administrators found themselves caught in the cross fire between college administrators, college faculties, budget planners, and state coordinating agencies. In 1973, David Bowman, dean of the school of education of the University of Wisconsin at Oshkosh, addressed the convention of the National Association of Laboratory Schools:

> I have been convinced for many years that campus laboratory schools have been convenient political footballs. To many politicians and central university or systemwide administrators, the campus school appears to be an ivy-covered and somewhat tarnished version of a modern elementary or secondary school that caters primarily to faculty members' children, and it represents a very visible and tempting example of how, by closing its doors, you supposedly save some dollars and force the use of elementary and secondary schools and at the same time cease catering to the children of the professionally elite. Well, as a taxpayer, I must question these kinds of naive judgments, particularly since, in our state, they are made by the same people whose judgments resulted in the placement of a university campus or branch campus in almost every city of moderate size in the state, to the point where the tax dollars are so dissipated there isn't a single institution that can have an adequate supply of resources to operate effectively. (Bowman 1973, 14)

Many laboratory schools labored in a variety of ways to convince the educational community of their viability. In some states they were able to have studies commissioned to examine laboratory schools. Excellent studies resulted in Wisconsin, Florida, Kansas, Hawaii, and New York.

Wisconsin, caught in a dilemma of its own making, according to Bowman, conducted a study chaired by McGeoch. Its first recommendation was that

> the responsible agencies endorse as policy the principle that each campus school will henceforth be considered individually in relation to its contribution to the program and purposes of the institution of which it is a part. This means that the future of each school would depend on institutional decision rather than on some external fiat concerning the value of campus schools in general. (McGeoch 1968, 39)

In spite of the suggestion that local decisions should determine the fate of campus schools, Wisconsin closed them.

In 1969, Florida conducted a similar study. The report recommended that "each of the campus laboratory schools now operating should be continued" (State University System of Florida 1969, 40). Six other recommendations intended to support and strengthen Florida's laboratory schools came out of the study. The laboratory schools remain in operation.

Also in 1969, Kansas completed a study of the laboratory school at Emporia State University (then Kansas State Teachers College). The report carried recommendations about functions, faculty, students, and costs. It concluded that

> the services of the laboratory school are not likely to be duplicated in local public schools because the latter have functions, objectives and responsibilities which do not parallel the needs of teacher education programs. Public schools are organized and administered to serve the needs of students and parents within a school district; laboratory schools are organized and administered to accommodate the needs of college teacher education programs.

The campus school at Emporia State University survives. It has recently entered into a collaborative arrangement with the local school district to achieve a secure future.

The University of Hawaii conducted a major study of its laboratory school in 1965. A shift of mission from teacher education to curriculum research and development provided the basis of support for preserving the school. (The final segment of Chapter 3 tells more.)

The story in New York is more complicated and its outcome less happy. A 1971 study, chaired by President E. K. Fretwell of the State University College at Buffalo, concluded that the schools were performing useful functions and should be continued. But struggles between SUNY's central coordinating body and budget officials led to another outcome. Buck (1975) described the steps taken to close the schools after the Fretwell Report. In 1976, Buck reported the outcome of the struggle. Lobbying by the leaders of the SUNY campus schools and the coalition they built moved the legislature to pass, without a dissenting vote, legislation to keep the schools open for an additional five years (Buck 1976). During that period, another study would ascertain the viability of future operations. The subsequent study in 1979 by Peterson examined two assumptions in the legislation:

1. The Learning Centers [campus schools] perform unique educational services for prospective teachers, school districts, and children; and
2. Essential aspects of research, demonstration and curriculum development can more effectively be provided in Campus Learning Centers.

The report concluded that the visiting evaluation teams found a good deal of evidence to support these two assumptions.

Not one of the eight conclusions of the Peterson study suggested that the schools be closed. After two major studies, it would seem that those desiring to close the schools (in this instance it appeared to be the Budget Office) would have let the matter rest.

Then events played into their hands. By 1980, New York State was suffering. The loss of industry, a mild recession, and decreased revenues required the state to reallocate its resources. At the same time, softness in demand for teachers made the campus learning centers a target. This time a more subtle approach was used to close seven of the nine remaining schools.

To entice cooperation, a plan was offered to administrators on SUNY's local campuses. Though the plan was not devised solely for the campus learning centers, they were most visible and most vulnerable. College presidents were told that for any programs they could trim or eliminate they could retain half the savings to allocate to other programs. The plan was met with skepticism, but the bait was taken—in good faith—particularly by newly appointed presidents. The outcome was a disaster.

The State University of New York is an overregulated system controlled by the Office of the Budget, the Legislature, and its own central administration. Constraints on the university system have been a problem since its formation. To address this problem, SUNY's chancellor, Clifton R. Wharton, Jr., and its board of trustees created an Independent Commission on the Future of the State University. Its report, *The Challenge and the Choice,* was completed in 1985. One issue examined was the budget officials' ploy. The commission's report described it:

> On the campuses the conviction is widespread that the fate of SUNY institutions depends on decisions by distant officials who are not charged with educational responsibility. This has produced an atmosphere of mistrust that complicates attempts by SUNY Central to encourage trimming of unnecessary programs. For example, SUNY's Chancellor reported to local campuses that the Director of the Budget had agreed to an incentive program for campuses that decided to trim or eliminate programs: the campus could be allowed to keep half of the resources thereby saved and reallocate them for the enrichment of other programs. The first test of this policy was the closing of several campus-based schools for faculty and community children, a measure agreed to with reluctance by some SUNY campuses after prolonged and painful discussion. In 1982–83, SUNY requested 40 of the 78 positions that had been allocated to campus schools be retained for other purposes. But the executive budget recommended retention of only 22 of those positions, later changed to 39. Then in 1983–84, all of the campus positions were eliminated.

Even two major studies of the campus schools, the second backed by legislation, did not alter the mind-set of those holding the purse strings. What happened in New York illustrates how external forces can not only influence but even control decisions on local institutions.

THE ROLE OF LEADERS IN THE DECLINE OF LABORATORY SCHOOLS

The principalship of a model school or a demonstration school was often an excellent route up the career ladder. In an address to the Laboratory School Administrators' Association, Goodlad (1971, 37) commented:

Perhaps too many of us have left the laboratory school to accept associate deanships, deanships or presidencies elsewhere, and it is interesting that the laboratory school has been a laboratory for the advancement to higher administrative posts.

Former principals promoted to administrative office might have been influential in assisting the schools by ameliorating, forestalling, or sidetracking efforts to close the schools or curtail their operation. They would also be in an ideal position to advise laboratory schools on new directions and to explain their vital role in teacher education. Perhaps many did. But they were in a difficult position. They had to accommodate internal politics in allocating resources. A former principal who allocated additional resources to a laboratory school or declined to make personnel cuts when others did might be accused of bias and favoritism. Thus an "ally" in the upper echelon was not necessarily helpful.

During the critical times of the 1960s and 1970s, laboratory schools faced a leadership crisis as their administrators moved up to staff the expanding multipurpose institutions. Few wanted to get involved in unpopular controversies or take a proactive stance on the schools' contributions. Timidity and insecurity rather than conviction often characterized their behavior.

Perhaps the most pungent commentary about leadership was made by William Van Til (1969, 13) in his address to the Laboratory School Administrators' Association:

> Strangely enough, the laboratory school sometimes has natural enemies within its own building—the laboratory school administrator who always accommodates and never leads.

In defense of such administrators it may be said that perhaps the beliefs nurtured by progressive education convinced laboratory school people there was nothing to worry about. But even as deliberate steps were being taken to make schools the central agents of change, the progressive movement itself was burning out. Because laboratory schools and their counterparts in education departments believed in the correctness of their approach, they neglected to rethink their purposes to meet new challenges. In 1980, John Goodlad commented on what happened:

Alas, once a laboratory school staff comes to know what is "best," more than a gentle persuasion is required to set it once more on the path of inquiry. The irony is that, from one perspective (and certainly from the viewpoint of staff satisfaction), demonstration of these tried and true practices is good. But perseveration in them, at the expense of trying what has not yet been tested, is not what laboratory schools are for. (Goodlad 1980, 48)

Goodlad's observation shows insight. Laboratory schools ought to be on the cutting edge of educational change. Yet neither laboratory schools nor education departments adjusted. Dewey's remarks in his last published essay apply:

Nothing is more reactionary in its consequences than the effort to live according to the ideas, principles, customs, habits or institutions which at some time in the past represented a change for the better but which in the present constitute factors in the problems confronting us. . . . New problems demand for their intelligent solution the projection of new purposes, new ends in view; and new ends necessitate the development of new means and measures. (Dewey 1952, viii, ix)

Except where unilateral decisions of legislatures or state education departments decreed their demise, laboratory schools that heeded the signs of the times made the adjustment and survived. Schools that failed to heed the signs and make appropriate changes closed.

THE ROLE OF MONEY IN THE DECLINE OF LABORATORY SCHOOLS

The shift of all or part of clinical teaching experiences to the public sector ultimately had a detrimental effect on laboratory schools. In competition for personnel and money they did not fare well. At best, they received no additional support. With inadequate funding, they found it difficult to provide clinical experiences, to conduct research, and to invent and test innovations. Schools that continued to do business as usual were eventually unable to show how they differed from public schools—a point not missed in internal or external studies.

Schools that were able to redirect their priorities did it by assuming extra workloads as well as by continuing to be all things to all people. Addressing this issue, John Goodlad (1971, 39) posed this rhetorical question:

> I don't have a nickel in my budget in the laboratory school at U.C.L.A. for innovation, experimentation, research. I have only a budget attached to teachers who teach children. Now how do you do experimentation and research under such circumstances?

Most laboratory schools still face this problem.

When a reason is given for closing a laboratory school, it is usually that the closing will save money. This is a fallacious but most appealing claim. Everyone loves to save money—except those whose ox is gored and those who have no chance to share in the spoils. After all, saving money shows accountability and fiscal restraint. But closing laboratory schools doesn't work that way. The funds for educating children, operating plants, and offering services continue but are lodged somewhere else.

Ninety percent of a laboratory school's budget goes into faculty salaries, administrative costs, and plant maintenance, including utilities. When a laboratory school closes and its children go to other schools, its budget appears to be available for other purposes, but it isn't. The state retains the funds and gives them to the school district where the children live. In only a few cases have funds from downsized or expired laboratory schools been retained by the university.

CRITICAL APPRAISAL

Even without the pressures of change, some laboratory schools would have closed. Many were too small to serve the college's expanding teacher education program or too ill-funded to develop alternative programs. Others simply were no longer performing useful functions in the college programs and were unwilling to change in order to do so.

Bowman (1973, 23) made the basic point succinctly: "It is difficult to justify the campus laboratory school if it does not uniquely serve the teacher education program." Faculty members in laboratory schools and in education departments developed role conflicts because they paid too little attention to this basic premise. Laboratory school teachers who saw teaching children as their primary job failed to see themselves first as "teachers of teachers." This perception deepened the gulf between the laboratory school and the education department, and professors began to feel unwelcome in their own institutions. The situation called for mediators to communicate the needs of each group and to build strategies for resolving the problems. The task should have been assumed by the schools' administrators. But many lacked the skills, failed to see this as their role, or had other agenda.

There have always been education professors who doubted the need for college-controlled campus laboratory schools, believing that support activities can better be carried on in the public schools. Educators in content fields are often less committed to the view that field experience is critical in preparing teachers. Smith (1980) suggested that educators in colleges of education should be held accountable for the inferior pedagogical training in their colleges and universities. But the problem has rarely been addressed, and it persists in clinical teaching sites.

Bringing theorists and practitioners together is an administrative challenge. Institutions able to accomplish it typically develop strong teacher preparation programs. Goodlad (1980, 49) offered sound advice:

> It is in the difference between persons selected to teach in laboratory schools and persons chosen for professional roles that the strength in collaboration lies. These two groups provide complementary, not overlapping, interests, skills and knowledge. Only when both groups come to recognize this can the problems posed by differing interests or values be resolved. But note, they are resolved not by choosing one over the other, but by employing them in an enterprise requiring, for successful progress, the joining of both kinds of expertise.

But theorists and practitioners have tended to isolate themselves rather than resolve their differences. Where this happened, the
laboratory school usually closed.

THE LABORATORY SCHOOL AS A UNIVERSITY RESOURCE

The laboratory school as a human resource must be useful not only to
programs of teacher education, research and development, and school
services but also to academic departments in the same way a
chemistry, physics, or computer laboratory is. The application of
knowledge by the learner in a setting that can be controlled and ma-
nipulated readily is vitally important. Schools of education share in
higher education's charter to push forward the frontiers of knowledge.
The laboratory school is where advancement in pedagogical practice
should be happening—especially in times of rapid social change. The
inability to meet the challenges of change has been lethal to many
laboratory schools. Tyler (1980, 5) identified these challenges for educational institutions:

> There are five kinds of changing conditions that seriously im-
> pact the work of schools and colleges today.
>
> 1. New groups of students are gaining access to educational
>   opportunity, groups that have not been effectively served
>   in the past.
> 2. New educational objectives are being formulated.
> 3. New problems and possibilities for education are arising
>   from the urbanization of society and the development of
>   large organizations responsible for schooling.
> 4. The out-of-school educational experiences are changing
>   rapidly; in most cases their constructive role is being
>   eroded.
> 5. New resources that may be exploited for educational tasks
>   are developing.

Because academicians, pedagogists, and practitioners can work
together under ideal conditions in a laboratory school, it is in a unique
position to investigate and offer possibilities for resolving educational

issues associated with the conditions Tyler identified. When this happens, the laboratory school becomes an integral part of the college's mission. It also does what Goodlad (1971, 40) claims it must do: "You justify a lab school by providing what the rest of American education is not providing."

The laboratory school's uniqueness is that it is free of the constraints that inhibit public schools: school boards, bureaucratic administrators, narrow curricular guidelines, and a charter that puts the education of children first. Goodlad (1980, 51) explained why public schools cannot undertake experimentation and innovation:

> Special demands, largely remedial, so inundate the schools today that hardly anyone ever considers anymore what a well-rounded comprehensive curriculum for all students might look like. The back-to-basics movement has virtually legitimized sterile, unimaginative teaching and reinforced textbooks and workbooks as the mainstay of elementary school instruction.

But a laboratory school is free to rearrange the curriculum, reassign personnel, restructure the delivery system, and reallocate resources. As an extension of the college, it can dare to undertake programs that public schools cannot attempt.

Because laboratory schools commonly have student bodies of volunteers, they can undertake missions and programs unlike those in regular schools. A 1974 report to the board of trustees of Ball State University by the Burris Laboratory School makes explicit the expectations for laboratory schools:

> A laboratory school is obliged to be different and to defend its variations from the norm. It is expected to venture beyond the usual limitations placed on public schools. Parents of children attending laboratory schools know and accept these conditions, being confident that innovation being carried out by competent professionals involves no undue risk for their children and has potential for real educational benefits.

John Goodlad, citing a former U.C.L.A. chancellor, advocates being direct with parents:

The function of this school is experimentation and innovation in education—the education of your children is a by-product. You send your children here in the same way you use the university hospital, and if you don't want your children involved in experimentation and innovation, you've got a public school next door, send your children there. (Goodlad 1971, 47–48)

Harsh as Goodlad's advice sounds, it is advice that must be heeded by the faculties and administrators of laboratory schools and colleges of education. A true laboratory pursues experimentation and innovation, and when its programs prove successful, it transfers them to the public sector and moves on to new issues.

To meet the challenges Tyler identified requires commitment and continuity on the part particularly of principals of surviving laboratory schools. Principals must select faculty, initiate programs, develop linkages with user departments, and lobby effectively for the schools' benefit. They must remain in their posts long enough to achieve stability and to sustain the impact of their programs. Unless they are ready to push on in spite of controversy and setbacks, their schools will not be on the cutting edge of educational change.

RETROSPECT AND PROSPECT

Probably no segment of higher education has been put under the microscope more often than laboratory schools. For schools that adapted it has been—and still is—a perpetual struggle. However, as in any time of transition, the survivors are stronger for the effort. In this sense, surviving laboratory schools offer evidence that the model is germane. Otherwise, why would major educational organizations now be advocating the formation of professional development schools to serve the functions traditionally served by laboratory schools?

This essay has addressed the problems laboratory schools have faced. The story has not ended happily for every such school. But it should not be inferred that surviving and new schools have a questionable future. For the efforts of dedicated laboratory school educators are being noticed. As this essay was being written, the Florida Legislature passed the Sidney Martin Developmental Research School

Act, which secures the operation of laboratory schools in the state and empowers other public universities to sponsor new schools.

New patterns of collaboration are emerging in Arizona, Alabama, and British Columbia. NALS representatives are assisting people in schools that have laboratory functions but no affiliation with a university. In some cases they are helping the schools to develop links with universities in their regions.

On the Navajo reservation in Tuba City, Arizona, Greyhills High School, a grant school under the Navajo Nation, is working in partnership with Northern Arizona University to start a center to improve schooling for Native Americans. The University Laboratory School in Hawaii is supporting this effort.

Even as this volume goes to press, educators in Texas and New Mexico are considering using laboratory schools in their teacher preparation programs.

Although change has spawned a crisis with dire consequences for some laboratory schools, it has challenged others, bringing fresh interest in their potential.

2

Functions of Laboratory Schools

Crayton L. Buck, Robert Hymer, Gene McDonald,
Jackson J. Martin, and Theodore S. Rodgers

THE CHANGING FUNCTIONS OF LABORATORY SCHOOLS

SINCE THE BEGINNING OF THE NORMAL SCHOOL MOVEMENT in the nineteenth century, laboratory schools in this country have performed important educational functions. Traditionally their commitment has been to assist in preparing teachers while delivering quality instructional programs for children attending the schools. Their initial functions in teacher preparation were demonstration, observation, participation, and student teaching. But over the years these functions have expanded to include preparing staff personnel, conducting research, developing curriculum, testing materials, providing clinical teaching experiences, serving special student populations, and participating in graduate assistant programs. By moving beyond their original roles, laboratory schools have not only responded to the changing needs of the teaching profession but have often led the way in improving the science and art of teaching.

The rationale undergirding each laboratory school is professional service to its educational community. The resulting local control enables each school to set priorities for contributing to the mission of

the parent institution. Inasmuch as higher education usually values innovation and experimentation coupled with community service, lab
schools can, with relatively few constraints, redirect their functions to
meet the challenges of the teaching profession.

The clients of a laboratory school have different needs and
expectations. The role of each laboratory school is influenced by the
priorities of its parent institution and by the creativity and leadership
of its own staff. Each school serves children, parents, college students,
college departments, and the teaching profession.

The evolution of laboratory school functions parallels the evolution of the parent institution. The metamorphosis of normal schools
into universities first set the stage for changes in laboratory schools. As
institutional purposes change, some laboratory school functions decline because of unclear policy direction, poor articulation, and be-
nign neglect from the parent institution.

Most laboratory schools continue to serve multiple functions.
An early study by Kelley (1964) ranked the functions as respondents
reported them: first, observation, then demonstration, student teaching,
research, participation, experimentation, and in-service education. By
1969, Howd and Browne noted a significant shift in the ordering of
functions. They concluded that

> the major change in role identification is in providing for re-
> search, experimentation and in-service education. The fact that
> slightly more than half the schools in the current study indi-
> cated that they either make a limited contribution or are not
> used at all for student teaching shows a marked change in role.
> (Howd and Browne 1970, 4)

In 1976, Duea surveyed administrators for their ranking of functions. He found this sequence: clinical experiences (observation and
participation), demonstration, research and development, in-service
training, and student teaching.

In 1987–1988, schools holding membership in the National
Association of Laboratory Schools (NALS) at any time during the previous three years were surveyed. Sixty-two schools responded, ranking

eight defined functions and estimating the percentage of effort they devoted to each (Johnson 1987; NALS 1988).

1. *Clinical teaching experience* generally refers to observation and participation in the activities of a class, but with less responsibility than during the practice-teaching period later in the program. Clinical experience is recommended throughout the full teacher education course. Some educators use this term to include all field activity, including practice and internship teaching.

2. *Curriculum development* refers to the design, crafting, and experimental use of curricula and supporting materials. A curriculum may be used in the school only for observation by college students and teachers from local schools, or it may be published and disseminated regionally, nationally, or even internationally.

3. *Observation* means occasional visits to a laboratory school to watch a particular lesson or teaching practice.

4. *Demonstration* is usually an arranged presentation of a lesson or educational practice, not necessarily distinguished from observation.

5. *Research* can mean any number of kinds of investigations, directed either by professors in the university or by the laboratory school staff itself.

6. *Staff development,* a fast-growing function, refers to formal training activities for teachers in local schools.

7. *Experimentation* can mean any of a number of preliminary innovations not qualifying as research or curriculum development.

8. *Student teaching* refers to the period when a prospective teacher takes rather complete control of a class under the supervision of the teacher and the college instructor.

Table I shows the functions in the order administrators ranked them in the 1987–1988 study. Table II shows the number of administrators ranking each function first.

TABLE I.
Laboratory School Functions
Ranked by Importance

Function	Rank
Clinical teaching experiences	1
Demonstration	2
Observation	3
Curriculum development	4
Research	5
Experimentation	6
Student teaching	7
Staff development	8
Other	9

N = 62

TABLE II.
Number of Schools Ranking
Each Function First

Function	Number
Clinical teaching experiences	25
Curriculum development	10
Observation	7
Research	5
Staff development	4
Demonstration	3
Experimentation	2
Student teaching	2
Other	4

N = 62

The rankings show significant changes between Duea's 1976 survey and the newer NALS survey. Curriculum development rose in importance; taken in combination with research, its rise demonstrates that schools have made substantial changes to accommodate the needs of their colleges and their regions. Curriculum development and research seem likely to continue to increase in importance.

Table III estimates the percentages of total activity devoted to various functions. Inasmuch as most schools do not engage in all eight activities cited, it should not be assumed that the total effort reported was congruent with the number of respondents.

TABLE III.
Percentage of Total Activity Devoted to
Each Function by Individual Schools

	0–9%	10–19%	20–29%	30–39%	40–49%	50–59%	60–69%	Over 70%
Clinical teaching experiences	7	11	7	5	3	6	4	5
Curriculum development	16	19	7	2	1	1		
Observation	16	4	12	1	2	2		
Research	24	17	3	3	1			
Staff development	27	10	4	1		1		
Demonstration	18	22	5	1				
Experimentation	21	13	2					
Student teaching	19	19	4	1		1		
Other	2	4		2	1	1		

Among functions reported but not listed in the survey were graduate practical programs, internships, and graduate assistant programs. This evidence coincides with a nationwide trend to bring into the teaching profession college graduates who were not education majors.

Many schools reported that they incorporate demonstration into staff development programs and in-service activities for teachers rather than just teaching model lessons for undergraduates.

On the evidence, it seems reasonable to infer that laboratory schools are taking on new functions in addition to traditional ones.

In the rest of this chapter we discuss and evaluate some of the important activities of laboratory schools.

CLINICAL TEACHING EXPERIENCES

Today, more than ever, teacher educators agree not only that clinical teaching experiences are crucial in preparing teachers but also that they should begin early in preparation programs, when they can complement the teaching of theory. Theory comes alive when it is applied in working with children in schools. And because clinical teaching experiences are most effective when they are planned and controlled, laboratory schools are particularly well suited to providing such services.

Many states mandate clinical teaching experiences for accrediting teacher education programs. The mandate assures that students have the opportunity to accomplish the objectives of methodology courses under the guidance of master teachers. Good practice in planning clinical teaching programs includes

- a planned series of carefully focused observations of instruction and classroom management practices for children of various ages.
- a planned tutoring program for individual students.
- a planned program of organized and executed mini-lessons.
- planned and executed series of lessons for small groups of children.
- planned and executed series of lessons for a whole class.
- planned and executed whole class units of teaching, with total responsibility for classroom management.

Clinical teaching experiences can be usefully subdivided into

- a pre-acceptance practicum (a stated number of hours of observation to be completed by candidates for teacher education before admission).
- an observation course (systematic observation experiences, followed by discussion and evaluation).

- practicum courses (clinical teaching experiences associated with methodology courses, required to give students practical experience and to prepare them to demonstrate mastery of the requisite concepts, skills, and methods associated with the course).
- an internship or student-teaching assignment (the culminating teaching experience, lasting from several weeks to a semester, during which the student, under supervision, integrates and applies knowledge and technique).

High standards in clinical teaching experiences require the kinds of settings that laboratory schools can provide. These schools are in a unique position to develop close working relationships with departments or colleges of education. This closeness fosters a partnership that makes coordination of services to prospective teachers effective. When clinical teaching programs are cooperatively developed by all who participate, there is no ambiguity about role functions, and high standards can be set and maintained by faculty and administrators responsible for preparing teachers.

When the college or university must turn to public schools as sites for field experiences, laboratory schools can serve as models. To assure the quality of clinical teaching experiences, agreements with public schools should include some safeguards:

- a written definition of the cooperative relationship, including its objectives, its procedures, and the roles of the participants
- a joint committee of faculty members and administrators from both institutions to monitor the agreement
- integration of clinical experiences with the college curriculum, including its concepts, skills, methods, and evaluation components
- guidelines for college or university staff members to follow when visiting the school to observe students
- a clear understanding of the level of preparation and experiential background required of teachers serving the program
- an agreement on the kind and amount of control to be exercised by the college or university

Clinical teaching is likely to remain a function of most laboratory schools. Many laboratory schools accept it as their primary mission, making them a first choice among school settings for this function.

RESEARCH AND DEVELOPMENT

Many commentators, particularly those outside academic circles, think of research in the narrow sense of following the "scientific method." In education, the stereotype most often takes the form of objective testing of control and experimental groups before and after competing treatments to establish which treatment—curricular, instructional, or organizational, for example—is optimal. This restrictive view is based on the hypothetico-deductive pattern, ostensibly borrowed from the experimental physical sciences. A typical piece of research in a common earlier version of this tradition might comprise a set of procedures for evaluating an educational program. St. Pierre (1979, 29) summarized the process:

> Program goals subject to evaluation are selected, success criteria are stated, measures are selected/constructed, an evaluation design is developed, treatment and comparison groups are formed, data are collected and analyzed, conclusions about the effectiveness of the program are drawn, and a report is written.

But the agenda of potential research efforts for laboratory schools is broader than St. Pierre's. Furthermore, the comparative method has been heavily criticized in current educational literature from two perspectives: philosophical and practical. Some of the strongest criticism has come from people who themselves have practiced educational research based on this paradigm. Even in the physical sciences, allegiance to the hypothetico-deductive pattern—the "scientific method"—has waned or vanished. Recent studies of what scientists actually do have shown little congruence between the steps dictated by the proclaimed scientific method and the procedures scientists follow in doing science. Thomas Kuhn and other noted philosophers and historians of science have questioned our notions of how science works and what scientific progress is.

Current educational research is being conceived in situational terms that are more qualitative and interactive than those subsumed within the hypothetico-deductive model. In view of such changes, what are some other kinds of educational research to which laboratory schools might profitably direct their attention?

Some have proposed that descriptive, historical, and theoretical studies are as authentic as experimental studies, and perhaps more useful. Others suggest that case studies and longitudinal studies are more appropriate for laboratory schools. Still others see these schools as developmental research centers for conceptualizing, developing, testing, and disseminating curricula. Another kind is policy research focusing on what can or ought to be accomplished in schools—a practical sort of research. And the spate of national reports on educational reform brought forth the proposal that laboratory schools offer themselves as "centers for experimentation, research, and evaluation needed for the implementation of some aspects of the national reports" (Van Til 1987, 23). Any—or all—of these proposals constitute potential research agendas for the nation's laboratory schools, based as they are in the everyday world of schooling but set in the theoretic environment of universities.

Most laboratory schools today engage, in varying degrees, in research or development. Their efforts range from action research conducted by a single teacher to major R&D projects conducted by teams. Among schools engaging in such research are Children's School at Carnegie Mellon University, Seeds University Elementary School at the University of California, Los Angeles, and the University Laboratory School at the University of Hawaii. The programs of these schools are presented in Chapter 3.

STAFF DEVELOPMENT

Reaching out to public schools to offer programs of staff development is a growing function of laboratory schools. Price Laboratory School at the University of Northern Iowa is an example. The goal of its program is to provide educational leadership for improving instructional strategies and materials for educational agencies in the area and for elementary and secondary schools across the state.

Price Laboratory School faculty members serve the profession by offering consultation, speaking services, staff development workshops, and course work. These activities are designed to relate theory to practice and to develop effective teaching strategies and materials for use by teachers.

By demonstrating its importance as an educational institution, this systematic approach brings visibility and credibility to the school. The collective impact of the faculty's achievement is evident in the many offices they hold in professional organizations, in the numerous presentations they make at local, state, and national meetings, in their authorship of published materials, and in the demand for the services they provide. These services are so widely used that nearly every county of the state is involved sometime during the school year.

SPECIAL EDUCATION

With the evolution of concern for special-education students over the past three decades, some laboratory schools began to deliver services to these students and their teachers. Among laboratory schools that have developed strong special-education components are the ones at the State University College at Buffalo (College Learning Laboratory), Indiana University of Pennsylvania (University School), and Illinois State University (Metcalf and University High). Children enter these programs through district or county committees on special education. The programs at these schools are organized and administered through collaborative agreements with multiple school districts, counties, or private agencies. The students enrolled are hampered by impairments of vision, hearing, or speech; by delays in language; by learning disabilities, mental retardation, or emotional disturbances; and by sundry physical afflictions, such as spina bifida and brain injury.

Each school maintains comprehensive educational programs to meet local needs and objectives. The academic curriculum is individualized. Whenever possible, children participate with their peers in nonsegregated classes. The school of State University College at Buffalo pioneered in mainstreaming brain-injured students. Similarly, the school at Indiana University of Pennsylvania developed an approach using resource rooms designed for students with a variety of impairments. The schools provide extra support for individualized educational programs (IEPs), using additional staff in occupational education, physical therapy, and related services required when the local committee on special education includes them in the IEPs.

Persons planning to teach in regular classrooms must learn how to cope with children with special needs. Experience with these students in clinical teaching is designed to make teachers more receptive to the needs of all learners. Viewing special education as a part of the total school program, not a separate entity, is characteristic of the educational offerings available in these schools.

Gallaudet College in Washington, D.C., operates two schools for hearing-impaired students—the Kendall Demonstration Elementary School and the Model Secondary School for the Deaf. Kendall School is a day school for the Washington, D.C., area; the Model School is a residential facility, and any student in the nation may apply for admission. Both schools operate under Congressional mandate (P.L. 91–587). The schools not only demonstrate methods of teaching hearing-impaired children but also develop, test, and evaluate methods and programs for use by their teachers. The Gallaudet schools search for answers, test theories, develop innovative practices, and find out what works and doesn't work.

SPECIAL–PURPOSE SCHOOLS

Many laboratory schools serve some gifted students, but University High at the University of Illinois, the laboratory schools at the University of Chicago, and the campus schools at Hunter College concentrate solely on the gifted. Students who enroll come from all walks of life and all socioeconomic backgrounds. Competition for entrance is rigorous because only a small proportion of applicants can be served.

Hunter, established in 1896, is one of the oldest schools for the intellectually gifted in the nation. Both schools maintain thorough, rigorous, innovative college-preparatory programs without neglecting the "whole person." Students are encouraged to participate in several interscholastic programs, including drama, art, music, and community education.

Gifted students are treated as persons who must be challenged with a curriculum that demands their best efforts. Classes are often marked by cooperative inquiry and lively interchange. Many students from University High and Hunter Campus High have earned high academic and societal awards, including the Nobel Prize and Wilson, Truman, Westinghouse, and National Merit scholarships.

Among the functions of laboratory schools, these schools also exemplify curriculum development, experimentation, demonstration, research, and dissemination of materials.

CONCLUSION

We have described some important but diverse functions of laboratory schools. No single school can serve them all simultaneously. But whatever set of functions they attempt, laboratory schools provide optimal environments for developing techniques of improving schooling in the United States. These schools have routinely reviewed and analyzed the art and science of teaching in their attempts to serve teacher education and to provide the best possible education programs for children. The impetus to do these tasks has not lessened; if anything, it is growing more intense.

3

Strategic Planning
for Laboratory Schools:
Concepts, Models, and Cases

THIS CHAPTER TELLS ABOUT THE FORMING of laboratory schools, giving their "creation stories"—or, more properly, their "re-creation stories," since their new designs were built upon older ones. We begin the chapter with an overview of laboratory school planning concepts to set the context for the stories that follow.

As a class, laboratory schools were created during a period of nationwide interest in and support of the idea that some schools were needed as sites for testing, demonstrating, or disseminating instructional innovations. Each lab school, however, has its own history of responding to the context of its sponsoring college, its locality, and its political climate. The accounts of seven schools, told by leaders heavily involved in their development, reveal common experiences in the re-creation of these schools. Ross A. Nielsen presents his account in the form of a blueprint for laboratory school development; Lynn McCarthy and Albert Bertani relate the generalized experience of two laboratory school leaders; Charles V. Branch, Adrianne Bank, Crayton L. Buck, Ann Baldwin Taylor, and Arthur R. King, Jr., analyze strategic planning as it evolved in their schools.

Strategic planning can be defined as "the effort to think creatively and systematically about planning for an organization, with emphasis on both internal factors and the external context of the institution." We believe that the stories related here can yield insight into the process of planning not only for laboratory schools but also for other schools related to university programs, such as professional development schools.

LABORATORY SCHOOL PLANNING CONCEPTS

The Niche

The niche, or slot, of the laboratory school in its larger institutional context is always of prime importance. A series of questions typify this element in planning: What is the laboratory school to do? Why will it do it? How will it do it? What alternatives must be considered? Is this type of service distinctive and necessary? Can the school do it well? Can the school get recognition for doing it well? Can it develop the support it needs? Who are its constituents?

The organizational base, usually in a college or university, often in a school system, sometimes in a partnership, is important. Will the base provide legitimacy? Support? Flexibility? Freedom? Resources?

The function and the organizational base help the school build a constituency and develop a set of connections. Among potential constituents are university colleagues in education and other knowledge fields, college and university administrators, local school systems, parents and students, teacher trainees past and present, legislators, businesses, professional organizations, funding bodies, and other organizations in the community with a stake in education.

The Resources

Resources make or break all programs, and laboratory schools almost universally have severe resource problems. A solid and predictable financial base makes possible the development of staff and the allocation of staff time to important teaching and nonteaching tasks, including research, publication, travel, conferencing, and other forms of networking.

The adequacy and appropriateness of staff is a prime concern of all laboratory school planners. Leaders must handle the usual functions of program direction, personnel development, finance, and communication, plus the important function of keeping the school visible in important circles in its environment.

Staff must be strong as teachers, and more. They often serve as researchers, writers, editors, teacher trainers, workshop leaders, and administrators of sections and projects.

Plant and equipment are important, too, although many schools prosper in spite of minimal, even substandard, plants and equipment.

Students

The types and numbers of students are crucial parts of the strategic plan. Students have been selected for lab schools by certain criteria, among them such specific features as age, handicap, ethnicity, giftedness, income, or socioeconomic class—and sometimes by ability and willingness to pay the costs. The types and numbers of students served often influence the financial health of the school. Students and their parents must accept the special mission of the school and the requirements imposed on them by that mission—experimentation, clinical teaching, demonstration, or other mission.

The strategic plan is a creative balance of these elements. The process of developing the plan is an interesting and important one, particular to the situation and the persons participating. In this chapter we illuminate the process.

LABORATORY SCHOOLS: BLUEPRINT FOR SUCCESS

Ross A. Nielsen, Professor Emeritus
University of Northern Iowa
Cedar Falls, Iowa

I plan to sketch for you a blueprint for laboratory school success. Although it would be satisfying to "start from scratch" to establish a school following these guidelines, most of us are unlikely to have that opportunity. However, each person having a relationship with a laboratory school, especially in an administrative role (principal, director, dean, department head) has an ongoing responsibility to place the school in increasingly strong positions on campus, in the community, and in the state—operationally, politically, and philosophically. Perhaps this plan can provide direction.

Although inherent circumstances on every campus limit what may be accomplished, I can assure you of the value and validity of the blueprint I present, and I urge you to consider each element thoughtfully as a potential key to strengthening your laboratory school. In doing so, remember as well that it is far better to create opportunities than to await them.

This blueprint is the culmination of a career committed to campus laboratory schools—thirty-nine years, the last twenty-four as director of what may be one of the nation's most productive laboratory schools. The plan is a seasoned one, polished during the past twenty years by the problems and successes of my own school and by the "big picture," or gestalt, that I constantly seek to generate by analyzing and synthesizing ever-changing forces, ideas, and trends from all areas and levels of education.

Campus laboratory schools have been operated and supported by teacher education institutions throughout the nation for more than a century. The school I served, Malcolm Price Laboratory School, began in 1883 as a "model school" serving Iowa State Normal School in the preparation of teachers. (Most normal schools later developed into teachers colleges for preparing educational personnel at both elementary and secondary levels.) Laboratory schools flourished first as "training schools" and then as "campus schools."

In the 1950s, the conditions that had favored campus schools began to change. Many schools were strangling in operational and philosophical webs that threatened their existence. Between 1960 and 1980, nearly half of the nation's laboratory schools were either closed or reduced in scope as they became caught in situations, frequently not of their own making, to which they were unable to respond.

The last decade, however, has been a period of relative stability. Some institutions have modified or closed their laboratory schools, but others have established new ones. Now there is an awakening interest in and recognition of the need for the unique contributions that laboratory schools can make to the professional preparation of teachers and to the quality of teacher education programs. It is imperative that the schools recognize this opportunity and prepare to capitalize on it. Founded on the new and expanding knowledge base of professional education, laboratory schools must structure clinical and laboratory experiences that will both serve as the foundation for and complement the study of theory in the professional curriculum.

Now, the blueprint. I identify and discuss five basic elements of the laboratory school structure: governance, school organization and program scope, staffing, student population and enrollment, and school and faculty roles and responsibilities.

Governance

The administrative status and governance structure established for the operation of a campus laboratory school are vital to its success. The school and its faculty can function best when

- the school has full department status within the college of education.
- the director of the school is also the department head, reporting directly to the dean of the college.
- the faculty has full university status, including probation/tenure appointments, faculty rank, research and sabbatical leaves, comparable salary and benefits, and opportunity to serve on college and university committees and to assume professorial roles.
- the school has a separate budget, as do other departments of the college and university.

- the school has a complete administrative staff, particularly school principals as needed, and assistance in administering the laboratory elements of teacher education.
- the school has a parent council that is limited to advisory status.

The governance element of the blueprint must be modified to fit the circumstances of each school.

School Organization and Program Scope

For optimal performance and success, the laboratory school must recognize its reason for existence. The university does not support and operate the school to educate elementary or secondary pupils. Rather, it operates the school to serve the university as a laboratory for programs that prepare educational personnel or to fulfill other responsibilities that the college or university assigns to the school.

This recognition of the school's purpose is crucial; it must be understood and accepted by faculty and administrators in the school and the university and by parents who enroll their children in the school. It does not mean that school students and their education are unimportant. It does properly identify priorities, putting into perspective the essential mission that justifies the laboratory school. The school carries unique, significant responsibilities to the university and the college of education. But the school must also offer strong programs of instruction for its students; otherwise it cannot be a strong laboratory for university students preparing to enter the education profession.

In its laboratory role, the school must serve all teacher preparation programs of the university. Thus, the pupil program ideally should span the years from pre-kindergarten through grade 12, including special education. The curriculum of the school, and its extracurricular program, should be comprehensive, providing instruction and services to fulfill simultaneously the educational needs of both school and university students.

The blueprint does not call for the school to be a "model school." Model schools made valuable contributions to elementary and secondary education in their time, but today a model school is not compatible with a teacher education laboratory—the significant role of the laboratory school. Nonetheless, the school as a teacher education laboratory can contribute significantly by exemplifying specific services, structures, and philosophies. Here are four examples:

- K–12 organization of the school by subject area, with each area chaired by a qualified member of the faculty, can present a model of program articulation valuable to both undergraduate and graduate students in teacher education.
- An exemplary school library and media center can enable prospective teachers to experience the value of such services to both teaching and learning.
- Exemplary guidance and health services at both elementary and secondary levels can provide prospective teachers the opportunity to study first-hand the contributions such programs make to a successful learning environment.
- An exemplary school philosophy, observable in the day-to-day operation of the school at all levels and in all elements of its program, can provide a solid foundation for laboratory experiences throughout the school.

Staffing

A major key to the success of the laboratory school is the nature and quality of its faculty. Clear expectations must be established for the faculty in the full range of responsibilities, including teaching both school pupils and university students, experimentation and research, writing and publication, and professional service.

Above all, faculty members must be warm, sensitive, and knowledgeable. They must represent the fullest possible range of cultures and classes. They must enjoy teaching and appreciate the unique opportunities in the laboratory school: to teach at both school and university levels, contributing simultaneously to the growth of students at both levels. They must be scholars of professional practice, keeping abreast of new developments and using such information to conduct action research in their instructional setting.

The relationship between faculty and administration must be open, positive, and supportive. The school must have a broad base of leadership from both faculty and administrators, and leadership must be exercised freely through mutual, informal cooperation. The more such leadership is generated, the greater the success of the school in fulfilling its complex role, leading in turn to a productive faculty and to heightened satisfaction and morale. This professional climate adds significantly to the generation of creative ideas within the school environment and to the success of the school and its faculty in other roles. Moreover, it is the key to attracting and holding strong, productive persons on the school faculty.

To function successfully in its complex array of professional responsibilities, the faculty must have adequate paraprofessional support, particularly in the elementary school, where the daily schedule puts a burden on teachers.

Student Population and Enrollment Policies

The school's role as a teacher education laboratory calls for enrolling the full range of student subjects. The student body must be multicultural, representing the whole population ethnically and socio-economically, and it must include the full range of student talents and abilities. The more comprehensive the laboratory school enrollment, the more realistically it can serve the full range of essential laboratory experiences.

School and Faculty Roles and Responsibilities

School and faculty success in assigned roles and responsibilities is a key element in the blueprint. Laboratory schools are primarily educational service units, established to provide a base in pedagogical experience for educational personnel. They are unique agencies in a position to make unique contributions to clinical knowledge and skill. But they can and must be more than that.

As an instructional unit within the university, the school imposes on its faculty members both the right and the responsibility to participate in each of the three professorial activities of the university: teaching, research, and professional service. Their contributions in research and professional service can be as singular as those they make in the areas of field experience traditionally served by laboratory schools. My blueprint calls for ongoing participation by the school and its faculty in all three kinds of activities, which I will discuss in turn.

1. Teacher education

From the days of the normal school, apprenticeship has been a constant feature of the preparation of teachers. Observing and learning from the "master teacher" in an ideal setting was the conceived role of the model school. Unfortunately, teacher educators have been unable to see the flaw in apprenticeship and to eliminate reliance on it as a philosophical base for teacher education programs. It is ironic that today, when new research is raising questions about our blind faith in apprentice-type, field-based experience and student teaching, these activities are being increased in programs of teacher education across the nation.

On the other hand, with the development and expansion of the new knowledge base in teacher education, the importance of clinical experience and the development of clinical knowledge and skills is gaining increased recognition. Early in this century, Dewey (1904) wrote that the primary function of student teaching should be to make the student more thoughtful rather than to gain immediate proficiency. He believed that the development of analytic skill would enable novices to judge their own work. In our time, such leaders in professional education as Smith (1983), Broudy (1985), and Berliner (1985) have addressed the value of clinical experiences in preparing classroom teachers. Rather than stressing practice, these leaders recommend attending to the development of skill in analysis, synthesis, reflection, and self-evaluation.

This orientation presents a rare and unusual opportunity for campus laboratory schools to make clinical laboratory experience a field of study, research, and development. My blueprint sets the highest priority on this element of the laboratory school's commitment.

2. Research, development, and dissemination

The blueprint requires faculty members to take advantage of the uniqueness of laboratory schools as a source of potential for productivity in research. Laboratory schools are where the action is, and applied action research, a fully legitimate endeavor, should be the byword.

The developmental activities I described in the section on teaching give the school faculty excellent opportunities to experiment and to do research on university students enrolled in clinical experience programs. In turn, faculty expertise in this area will enable the faculty to disseminate the new knowledge and skills to other field experience centers used by the university.

Product-oriented research and development offers the school faculty another wide array of opportunities. Contributions can enhance the laboratory school in a number of ways:

- Research in school curriculum and instructional processes engages the faculty in the study and development of new knowledge, invigorating both the faculty and the school program.
- Opportunities arise to develop cooperative research with other university departments, enriching both the laboratory school's programs and its on-campus status.
- Testing and evaluating programs and demonstrating ways of teaching afford opportunities to engage elementary or secondary schools throughout the state, yielding both recognition and improved relations.
- Disseminating research-based materials brings gratification to faculty and esteem to the laboratory school.

Only laboratory schools in a university setting, operating in the modes presented here, are in a position to function effectively in the area of product-oriented research. My blueprint includes this effort in the design of a successful laboratory school.

3.   Professional service

The school and its faculty operate simultaneously in the worlds of the university and the public schools. This dual role gives the school an extraordinary opportunity to provide service and leadership to the state. The business of the laboratory school focuses regularly on teacher education, on elementary and secondary school teaching and curriculum, and on research and development in curriculum and instruction. These activities relate directly to ongoing activity in every school in the land in search of program improvement.

Despite the potential burden, faculty members must also be available for professional service to the department, the college, and the university in the ongoing deliberations of committees, councils, and other faculty bodies. Such efforts, though time-consuming, enable the laboratory school to contribute its fair share of participation, to interject a unique perspective, and to build linkages that strengthen both the mission and the functions of the school.

The blueprint requires a commitment to professional service by the school and its faculty through contributions to an extensive array of activities:

- On campus. Sponsoring conferences; offering workshops; cooperating with faculty colleagues in course and project development; serving as resource teachers or consultants; writing and publishing; teaching special courses or classes; participating in college and university affairs; serving on committees, councils, and other university bodies; and participating in professional associations.
- Off campus. Sponsoring conferences; offering workshops; directing in-service programs; teaching extension classes; writing and publishing; providing leadership to elementary and secondary schools and teacher education through professional associations; giving papers and presentations; serving on educational boards, councils, and committees; acting as resource persons or consultants by engaging in research and development activities as a professional service.

Summary

I have presented a blueprint for laboratory school success. There are other designs, and every school must, in the long run, build its own design to fulfill its mission. You should know, however, that the blueprint I have sketched is a proven one, derived from the operation, roles, and achievements of Price Laboratory School and its energetic, productive faculty. I suggest that you study this design, consider its significant elements, and identify the ones that may present an attractive modification or addition to your own laboratory school.

Recently Haberman (1985, 57) predicted that "laboratory schools will be resurrected as special mission elementary and/or secondary schools" and that "the 'new' laboratory schools will generate a literature of applied, action research on the day-to-day problems of teachers and schooling." In calling for the creation of pedagogical laboratories, Berliner (1985, 6) said, "We need real laboratories in education, just as do chemists, biologists, and physicists, who also must learn to experiment while they are in training." And Broudy (1985, 38), in proposing the elements of professional studies, wrote, "It would be highly desirable for courses in education wherever suitable to incorporate the analogue of the laboratory."

I believe that laboratory schools will accept this challenge to create professionally stimulating, purposeful laboratories for pedagogical education. As they remodel for this effort, the schools must look to the keystone of the structure: leadership, the essential element that serves all others and holds them in place. I urge you to both provide and develop leadership to serve the roles and responsibilities I have discussed for laboratory schools, and to extend that effort to assist your institution in designing and building an enlightened teacher education program based on the modern conception of laboratory experiences.

LABORATORY SCHOOLS IN TRANSITION

Lynn McCarthy and Albert Bertani
National College of Education
Evanston, Illinois

Laboratory schools must renew and reevaluate their mission and role in education. They need a clearly articulated mission to position themselves within the larger context of the college and university. Their mission may take a number of directions: research, curriculum development, collaborative work with public schools, providing clinical sites for teacher preparation, serving as model schools, and concentrating on staff development.

The first step in defining a mission is conducting a resource audit to identify strengths and weaknesses and develop a profile of the school and its resources. From the profile the school can determine whether its mission corresponds to the requirements of the people and agencies it serves, both internally and externally.

Administrators and faculty who assess the mission and role of the laboratory school must define their criteria. Evaluation should center on the elements that research has shown to make for effective schools. These elements can serve as organizers for the planning and evaluation effort.

Self-Study and Evaluation

Any self-study and evaluation effort must deal with environmental issues associated with the laboratory school. Environmental scans must include study and evaluation of both internal and external factors affecting the school. A model for self-study and evaluation should include the following components: climate, culture, and functions of the laboratory school; mission and role of the laboratory school as related to the school, college, or department of education; relationship with the school, college, or department of education; and links to connect the present with the future.

The study should begin with understanding what the school does. It should include the influence of the sponsoring university or college and other outside forces, along with the influence of inside factors—cultural elements, policies, and practices that have become established within the school. Such factors may not have been openly discussed or made part of written policy or statement of mission, yet they embody implicit values that strongly influence the organization.

The following structure is proposed as a guide for conducting a self-study that includes the school's functions, its mission, and its relationship with the school of education. The structure is not all-inclusive, and it must be tailored to the organization under review.

Step 1. Detail the functions of the laboratory school.

How do faculty members spend their time? What do they do in addition to teaching? As the functions are listed, examine how each one has changed in the past five to ten years. Has there been a shift in focus over the years? Was the shift predetermined by the school staff (faculty and administration), or was it a response to pressures and other influences? If the latter, what were the sources of these pressures and influences? How is the morale of the staff? Does the staff feel a connection with the entire university or college community? With local schools? With other special schools, including other laboratory schools?

Step 2.   Determine how the laboratory school is unique.

How does it differ from the public schools in the area? What types of instruction are used that are not used in other schools? Examples might include instruction in writing using methods drawn from recent research on writing, teaching reading through trade books, and innovative methods of instruction in math, science, or music. Examine strengths and weaknesses as part of the process.

Step 3.   Interview parents, college and university constituents, and public school personnel to find their perceptions of the laboratory school.

Note the relationships between external and internal perceptions of the laboratory school. Conduct a follow-up study of children once served by the laboratory school to determine what paths they have taken since leaving.

Step 4.   Identify exemplary programs within the school.

What classifies these programs as exemplary? Have they received appropriate recognition? What hinders their implementation in other schools? How are exemplary programs recognized and disseminated?

Step 5.   Relate the mission of the laboratory school to the larger mission of the college and university.

Review the strategic plans of the college and the university. Interview the president, provost, dean, and key faculty members in the community. Find out how the college or university plans to influence education in the community, state, and nation.

Step 6. Assess the school's relationship with the school or college of education.

What is the laboratory school's relationship with the school or college of education? How does the laboratory school complement the mission and direction of the college? How does it help bring "fame and fortune" to the college? What prevents the fulfillment of its mission? What strengths does the laboratory school have that bring the college closer to its mission? In what manner does the school or college of education provide for and recognize the contributions of the laboratory school?

Step 7. Set future directions.

The laboratory school should revise its major goals and objectives and develop a clear mission statement. Next, sufficient resources must be directed toward the priorities to ensure their success. If the laboratory school is to redirect its future, it must find ways to link the present with the future.

If the laboratory school is to be integrated within the college or university, their missions must be compatible. Do the functions of the laboratory school complement the mission of the school of education? What major thrust of the laboratory school will make it more noticeable and more identifiable? What is being done now that (a) should continue, (b) should be eliminated, (c) should be reduced, or (d) should be expanded within the next five years to make the laboratory school more successful? What resources are needed for success?

Potential Missions of a Laboratory School

1. Research

Laboratory schools have the capacity to conduct longitudinal research because they have a stable student body. They should study the results of innovations through quantitative and qualitative evaluation methods. Such studies can reveal the long-term effects of a specific type of instruction that cannot be adequately evaluated in other settings.

2. Curriculum development

Laboratory school faculty members are creative people who can develop materials that translate research findings and new methods into classroom practices. Although research in many content areas is growing by leaps and bounds, its application to instruction lags far behind. Laboratory schools can fulfill an important role in bridging theory and research to daily practice. If others are to benefit from their creativity, faculty members must publish their findings in teaching journals and participate in conferences that introduce new materials and methods of instruction to other educators.

3. Collaboration with public schools

Laboratory school faculty members and their colleagues in public schools can work together to develop new theories and methods of instruction. Collaboration enables both to benefit from differing views and teaching experiences. Collaborative efforts can also be initiated with private schools, other laboratory schools, and community agencies offering human services. Faculty from schools around the country or within a state can share ideas, develop research projects, and initiate innovative curriculum practices.

4. Clinical services

Almost all laboratory schools have a role in preparing future teachers. Teacher preparation takes different forms, including staff development for teachers, developing internships, and initiating five-year programs. A well-planned and well-designed program to initiate beginning teachers into the profession is vital if the profession is to meet the demands of the public.

5. Model schools

When outstanding teaching faculty develop new instructional materials and methods, the laboratory school can become a model of instruction, a place where people concerned with schooling can observe new practices.

Laboratory school faculties also have the opportunity to share ideas and methods with their public school counterparts. Although it is sometimes difficult to begin to consult through school districts, some teachers can pave the way in opening opportunities for colleagues.

Laboratory schools can also model the roles of teachers as teachers/writers, teachers/researchers, or teachers/clinicians who, in their combined roles, provide resources for the children and the school community as a whole.

6. Staff development and in-service training

Laboratory school faculty members can share their expertise with experienced teachers by inviting them to spend time in the laboratory school. Conversely, laboratory school faculty members can go into public schools for the same purpose.

Conclusion

All institutions go through cycles of transition to new developmental periods. It is time now for laboratory schools to determine their purpose and direction and take charge of their own destiny. Only through self-determination can they become more influential in teacher training and other educational development processes.

COLLABORATIVE LABORATORY SCHOOLS: A POSSIBLE MODEL FOR THE FUTURE

Charles V. Branch
Metropolitan State College
Denver, Colorado

Those of us participating in the quest to improve the quality of education at all levels understand the importance of quality field-based experiences for pre-service teachers.

Many state boards and departments of education and university-based schools, colleges, or departments of education are requiring more and earlier field-based experiences in teacher-training programs. But too often those "more and earlier field-based experiences" are simply more of what has not been very effective: unplanned, unsupervised, uncontrolled, haphazard exposure to youngsters being taught by a so-called master teacher in a nonexperimental classroom environment. Most of us who have been intimately involved with laboratory schools know the importance of field-based experiences that are planned, supervised, controlled, and evaluated and that involve teacher trainees directly with many and varied teaching/learning activities in an experimental environment. Further, most of us believe that master teachers must know the theoretical basis for their teaching behavior and be able to communicate it. Some of us even believe that laboratory schools are the key to dynamically improving the quality of future teachers and, through them, the quality of education at all levels, including the faculties of teacher education institutions.

I believe that in the near future it will be necessary for every school of education to have at least one laboratory school to educate new teachers to the level of competence demanded by our society. But as is often the case in education, adequate funding probably will not be provided by legislatures or institutions of higher education to establish or reestablish a traditional university-owned and -operated laboratory school.

One solution is to establish laboratory schools in cooperation with public school systems. This article tells how a public school in Denver, Greenlee Elementary School, was converted into a cooperative laboratory school called Greenlee/Metro Laboratory School.

The school is four blocks south of the Auraria Higher Education Center in downtown Denver. It has been cooperatively operated by the Denver public school system and the school of education of Metro State College since 1982. The school has 441 children enrolled, from early-childhood classes to grade 3.

The student body consists of students from a depressed socioeconomic neighborhood plus students bused in from middle-class and upper-middle-class homes. Culturally and ethnically, the students represent the diversity of the community, as do the members of the faculty.

The cooperative laboratory school is an outcome of the commitment and hard work of many people dedicated to improving the quality of education at all levels. The motto of the school is "Working together for excellence."

The cooperative effort began in 1981, when I was asked to assist the Denver public schools in designing a magnet K–6 laboratory school, to be one of several unique magnet schools of the Total Access Plan. The purpose of the plan was to eliminate forced busing in Denver public schools. The plan was presented to the court involved, which studied it and ultimately rejected it. Soon after the plan was rejected, administrators from the Denver school system and Metro State College decided that the cooperative laboratory school was so important that it should be developed anyway.

The initial developmental step was for the superintendent of schools, the president of Metro State College, and the dean of Metro's school of education to agree on who would be responsible for what. The school system agreed to continue support for faculty, staff, and administrative salaries and for current instructional and noninstructional costs, including the transportation of students.

It was agreed that the school would have more autonomy than other schools in the system, in order to fulfill its role as a laboratory school. Metro State College agreed to employ a full-time coordinator of pre–student-teaching experiences for college students, who would be housed at the laboratory school. Further, it was agreed that intermediate, middle, and high schools would be developed after the first one was operational. This part of the original agreement is yet to be realized.

Next, meetings were held with the public school teachers and the faculty of the MSC school of education to discuss the benefits and liabilities of the cooperative effort. Also discussed were the significant increases in workload, the need for teachers, and the opportunities to become master teachers and teacher educators. Participation in the cooperative effort was voluntary for both faculties.

During the same period, the superintendent of schools was working with the board and his administrative staff to build support for the cooperative effort. The principal and the dean were simultaneously meeting with groups of community leaders, political powers, and parents to gain support for the cooperative endeavor.

Of equal importance was the formation of the Laboratory School Advising Council. The council was originally made up of four public school teachers, four school of education faculty members, the PTSA president, the chairperson of the School Improvement and Accountability Committee, the principal, the assistant superintendent for elementary education, and the dean. The council was formulated as a mini-school board. Its major assignment was to develop the laboratory school's goals, objectives, policies, procedures, and faculty development program, but its most important function was to build trust and respect among the two faculty groups. The council established the following goals for the cooperative laboratory school:

• to provide more effective education for Greenlee Elementary School pupils
• to provide more effective education for school of education students
• to provide professional development and collaborative opportunities for both faculties
• to use fully the available resources of the Auraria and Greenlee campus and communities

The council established policies and procedures to attain these goals. Two of the most important were the administrative structure and procedures for conducting research in the laboratory school. The council makes recommendations to the principal and director of laboratory schools (formerly the coordinator of pre–student-teaching experiences). The principal and the director make decisions within the existing policies and procedures of the school system and the college. In other instances, the dean and assistant superintendent make the decisions. The council acts as a clearinghouse for all research and activities to be conducted in the laboratory school.

Since the cooperative effort began, a number of changes have been made. Most significant were personnel changes. A new coordinator (director of laboratory schools) was appointed. The original principal retired. His successor was later promoted to the central administrative staff and was replaced by the current principal. Six laboratory school faculty changes were made this year. The school's name was changed from Greenlee Elementary School to Greenlee/Metro Laboratory School. Over $140,000 was spent on refurbishing the school building, including classroom carpeting.

Data indicate that the cooperative laboratory school is working. For example, during the first semester of operation, only 4 MSC faculty members, 21 teacher trainees, and 4 public school faculty members participated in long-term activities. After two years, the numbers were up to 12 MSC faculty members, 145 teacher trainees, and 11 public school teachers. Other indicators of success include improved faculty morale; the addition of a science and mathematics laboratory; a broader base of support from parents, the community, faculties, and administrators; and increased trust, openness, and respect among all parties. Research and curriculum development projects, programs for parents, and faculty development activities also have increased. Teacher education courses, seminars, and in-service workshops now are being conducted in the laboratory school as well.

The continuing successes of the laboratory school provide the basis for its long-range goals, which are

- to become a staff development center for public school personnel.
- to become an applied research/experimentation center to improve teaching/learning.
- to become a K–6 magnet school.
- to become a training center for bilingual teachers.
- to become a real community school providing extended day learning opportunities for children, parents, and community.

This school's successes have further reinforced my belief that laboratory schools are the key to dynamically improving the quality of education at all levels and that every teacher education institution will need such a school to educate and train a new kind of teacher. I further believe that laboratory schools developed and operated cooperatively with public schools may be able to contribute more to improving education at all levels than a traditional university-owned and -operated laboratory school can.

In summary, I believe that the most important ingredients needed for establishing a collaborative laboratory with public schools are these:

- a positive working relationship between the local school system and the teacher education institution

- a majority of the teacher education faculty who are committed to field-based experiences for teacher trainees
- a majority of teacher education faculty who believe they can learn from public school teachers, and vice versa
- a public school faculty willing to do more than is required by any negotiated contract agreement
- a principal who is committed, competent, and able to function as a member of an administrative team
- a college coordinator who is respected by the principal, public school teachers, parents, teacher educators, teacher trainees, and college faculty members across the campus
- a laboratory school advisory council composed of respected leaders from both faculties
- parent, community, and political support
- administrative and board support
- at least one key public school central administrator who supports research and experimentation
- a great deal of patience and understanding

SEEDS UNIVERSITY ELEMENTARY SCHOOL

Adrianne Bank
University of California at Los Angeles

During the Corinne A. Seeds era (1925–1957), the University Elementary School was an outstanding example of John Dewey-oriented progressive education. That is, children were not just learning basic skills in preparation for the next educational step; they were experiencing intellectual and social life and learning by reflecting on it as it was happening. Theory and practice generated in the University Elementary School shaped the training of a strong group of teachers, influenced educational practice in the region for a number of decades, and fostered the building of the California Framework for Elementary Education.

During the 1960s and 1970s, John Goodlad, dean of the U.C.L.A. Graduate School of Education and director of the University Elementary School (UES), focused educators' attention on the nongraded, team-taught school structure operating at the school. At the same time, Madeline Hunter, as principal, encouraged teachers to use her principles of effective instruction in the classroom.

For about forty years, then, UES was primarily a demonstration school showing how innovative ideas could be carried out in an elementary school with a group of 450 children selected to represent the diversity of ethnicity, income, and abilities of the city's population.

In the early 1970s, Madeline Hunter began to call for a redirection of energies in laboratory schools in general and in UES in particular. Of laboratory school functions, Hunter (1970, 14) said:

> The laboratory school must shed its role as a demonstration and training installation inducting novitiates into accepted and traditional practice. It must become a center for inquiry, an essential component of the educational design to produce new theory, to translate that theory into generalizable practice, to disseminate that knowledge and practice into the mainstream of American education, and to develop vigorous leaders.

To make the school a center of inquiry, she saw as essential

- the recognition of appropriate roles.
- the development of interrelationships.
- the appointment of appropriate staff.
- the registration of a heterogeneous student body.
- the provision of adequate facilities and budget.

Within the last several years, UES has moved to implement these proposals. This movement has become possible and desirable for a variety of reasons. The university and its graduate school of education have become increasingly interested in establishing links between academic research and real-world problems. Dizzying demographic, social, and technological changes in Los Angeles are rippling through the schools, and the educational reform movement is sparking the search for ways to solve problems. Finally, the background and interests of Director Richard C. Williams, not only as a professor of administration but also as past president of a local school board, have accelerated the shift in direction of the UES.

Under Williams's direction, the school is moving to assume leadership in three prime areas of educational need—wellness, technology, and continuous day care—while it continues to model alternative curricular practices and structures for visitors. Essential to the school's agenda is the integration of research, development, evaluation, and dissemination.

Through a combination of means—analysis of needs and trends, discussions with educators and makers of educational policy, and exercise of staff interests and skills—UES identified the three topics around which to organize theoretical and practical inquiry:

• Wellness. How can schools promote the physical, social, and emotional health of young children to enable them to cope now and in the future with the problems of a turbulent, changing society?
• Technology. How might computers be integrated with classroom practices to directly enhance learning and be coordinated with instructional management and administrative systems to document students' progress and their need for remediation and enrichment?
• Continuous day. How might school and day-care programs be conceived, operated, and funded to provide the combined emotional and social supports needed by children away from home all day?

For each topic, UES organizes a parallel set of activities. The staff first develops a long-term vision for its own students and those in public schools in Los Angeles. UES is helped in this endeavor by a sister public school in a low-income minority community committed to the same educational goals. Then a long-range plan is developed, which identifies issues to be addressed, along with related activities or events. A research agenda, a dissemination strategy, and staffing and budgeting plans are formulated.

UES has initiated fund-raising efforts to supplement its regular budget. Funding sources include parents, alumni, foundations, and "Friends of UES." The funds are used to support a part-time project manager, to provide released time for teachers, to employ consultants, to mount and participate in conferences, and to develop such products as articles, brochures, instructional materials, and training manuals.

Faculty members from university schools and departments participate in conceptualizing and carrying out research efforts. For example, staff members from the schools of education, management, medicine, and public health join efforts related to wellness. In technology, relationships with industry (for hardware, software, and technical assistance) and with U.C.L.A.'s computer science department have been developed. Child care and academic integration for a continuous day are concerns of many state and local agencies, and continuous-day plans are being developed to involve these agencies, along with day-care providers and trainers of day-care providers.

Research and inquiry have always been hallmarks of the UES laboratory school. Now research is becoming more integrated and more closely related to general school and social issues.

COLLEGE LEARNING LABORATORY: A MODEL OF A COOPERATIVE LEARNING SCHOOL

Crayton L. Buck
State University College
Buffalo, New York

Present Functions and Organization of the School

The current functions of the College Learning Laboratory, in descending order of commitment of attention and resources, are clinical teaching experiences, observation, research, and curriculum development. The primary mission of the laboratory school is to serve as a major field center for students aspiring to become teachers of elementary school students and special-education students. A major emphasis is the development and use of a preparation model for graduate students aimed at fostering a career orientation to teaching, particularly in special education.

The school is a voluntary participant in the court-ordered school integration magnet program, which features a close working relationship with the Buffalo school district. Seventeen other school districts send typical and atypical children to the school, either through the Committee on Special Education or through the voluntary choice of parents.

About eight hundred students are enrolled, from ages two through fifteen. There are a toddler class, a class for three-year-olds, three sections each of pre-kindergartners through eighth-graders, and nine self-contained special-education classes. Instruction for learning-disabled students occurs in resource rooms. Nearly a hundred speech-impaired or language-delayed students are among the school's students.

The State University of New York (SUNY) provides 50 percent of the faculty, all the buildings, and all costs for maintenance, heat, light, and repairs. The Buffalo school district provides 50 percent of the faculty and matches the instructional budget provided by the state.

Planning the School Program: A Developmental History

The school has a tradition of serving teacher education programs, primarily through pre–student-teaching activities, including observation and participation. In 1962, admission policies changed to insure equal accessibility. By 1977, the population had switched from almost all Caucasian students to over half minority students.

In the 1960s and early 1970s, the increasing emphasis on special education prompted the establishment of a special-education component to the school.

Throughout the decade from 1966 to 1976, the state's budget office in Albany mounted efforts to close all campus-based laboratory schools in the state. Extensive lobbying kept the schools open, but by 1977 their future was tenuous, at best.

These events provided the impetus for the school and college to search for alternatives. At the same time, the City of Buffalo was ordered to develop a plan to insure that the schools would be desegregated. When the school district developed its program of magnet schools, discussions were held with the college to ascertain whether the Learning Laboratory should be a partner. Many stimuli focused simultaneously to insure discussion and follow-through. The most powerful stimulus was the desire for the survival of the Learning Laboratory.

A new plan for change was administratively and legislatively arranged. Furthermore, the school was included in a court order that insured its permanence, a new and attractive condition for the school. A formal agreement was made among all parties, including the president, the vice-president, and the dean at the State University College, Buffalo; the director of the College Learning Laboratory; the superintendent and associate superintendent for instruction of the Buffalo school district; and the federal judge with jurisdictional responsibility for the desegregation plan. Key legislative leaders from the local constituencies participated at the political level.

The change brought no new missions to the Learning Laboratory. The revised design of its program was influenced by the local priority to desegregate the schools. The college's need to meet standards of the National Council for Accreditation of Teacher Education in education, special education, and urban education became a reality through the collaborative arrangement.

Responses to the New Design

The response to the new design can only be described as enthusiastic. All parties put forth tremendous effort to initiate the agreement. People involved in its implementation worked for many years afterward to make the school function effectively. Care and attention were given to resolving issues that surfaced from the integration of personnel from competing unions. In the process, establishing a strong commitment to laboratory school education with a magnet school orientation was critical to success.

Parents and students were, and have remained, enthusiastic. The College Learning Laboratory/Campus West is one of the more popular choices for enrollment in the city and the region. The admission criteria did not change, and the student body still consists of volunteers. Admission is governed by a lottery system designed to insure that the majority/minority ratio in the school reflects that of the city and region. To insure a heterogeneous population, the enrollment of special-education students is offset by the admission of gifted and talented students, who constitute 10 to 15 percent of the school's enrollment.

The College Learning Laboratory became a voluntary participant in the desegregation program for the Buffalo school district in

1977. The success of the school in integrating students from all walks of life has made the school a model worth emulating.

Unanticipated Results of the Change

The agreement among the participating parties provided amply for operating the school. But some issues could not be anticipated because disparate union contracts govern the two faculties. State employees are organized under the United University Professions (UUP), an affiliate of the American Federation of Labor. The UUP contract is collegially based and rooted in the idealistic orientation exhibited in higher education. In contrast, teachers in the school system are with the Buffalo Teachers Federation (BTF), an affiliate of the National Education Association. The BTF contract reflects the strong blue-collar work ethic associated with the industrial orientation of a major manufacturing city. The contract is rooted in realism, concreteness, and specificity to the point of crossing *t*'s and dotting *i*'s. When the school was formed, it was hoped that there would be few difficulties with working conditions. However, a constant balancing act is required for maintaining focus on the school's mission.

Operating a laboratory school requires faculty committed to the preparation of teachers. Persons recruited as state faculty understand this when they are hired, and they are held to it during the review for retention. But the same commitment does not always characterize faculty employed by the city's board of education. Even though the conditions for teaching are explained, teachers do not always embrace them in practice. Fortunately, the majority of the public school faculty are committed to laboratory school education. However, it is difficult to remove a teacher whose accountability is to an agency other than the college.

Future Changes

The College Learning Laboratory/Campus West achieves change through its commitment to accreditation by the Assembly of Elementary Schools, Middle States Association. Accreditation requires extensive self-study and introspection, and the required periodic reviews provide the challenge for change and renewal. Thus reassessment of current practices and the charting of new directions is an ongoing process.

Looking toward the future, the College Learning Laboratory will probably focus on electronic classrooms, distance learning, and networking associated with technological advances. The school will continue to stress its service function as an exemplary center for the preservice education of prospective teachers. Initiatives for collaborative ventures in research and curriculum development will continue.

A LABORATORY SCHOOL FOR
DEVELOPMENTAL RESEARCH IN PSYCHOLOGY

Ann Baldwin Taylor
Carnegie Mellon University
Pittsburgh, Pennsylvania

Carnegie Mellon University Children's School is located in the Margaret Morrison Building of the Carnegie Mellon University campus in Pittsburgh. It focuses on early-childhood education for students from three to six. The school has a capacity of a hundred children, who are scheduled by age: three- and four-year-olds attend half-day sessions; five- and six-year-olds attend full-day sessions. The school strives to maintain a diverse yet balanced student population. Each class comprises students from various ethnic and socioeconomic backgrounds who are at different stages of personal development. The staff consists of eight certified early education instructors and two administrators, who teach and direct the school.

Mission

Sponsored by Carnegie Mellon's department of psychology, the Children's School is a multifaceted facility. It offers research opportunities in child development and growth to faculty and students of psychology, and it provides opportunities for professional training in early education by serving as a field experience site for teacher certification candidates in the Carnegie Mellon/Chatham College Teacher Education Program. At the same time, the school creates a unique educational and social experience for its students and serves as a model and resource for parents and educators. Like Carnegie Mellon University itself, the Children's School aims to create knowledge through research, to disseminate information from research, and to apply research in actual practice.

The Children's School and Teacher Education

For the past twenty years, Carnegie Mellon University and Chatham College have had a unique cooperative program to prepare early-childhood and elementary teachers. The principal focus of the program has been to produce effective teachers for urban schools in the context of a liberal arts education.

More than a decade ago, the program introduced a weekly required, supervised half-day field experience in a classroom, to accompany and augment the academic and theoretical material in education courses. Prospective teachers learn to use technology in a variety of ways, including the videotaping and viewing of microteaching (classroom teaching simulations).

With the advent of the microcomputer, the joint program has developed an experimental learning module about microcomputers as part of the sequence of courses required for teacher certification.

The Children's School and Early-Childhood Research

The Children's School is a laboratory for research, design, development, and evaluation of curriculum. But it also offers opportunities for developmental psychologists from the university and the college to study the development of young children.

For some research and training programs, observers in the classrooms or behind one-way mirrors in the observation booth record selected aspects of children's freely occurring play, social interactions, and use of materials. For other research programs, children are asked if they would like to go, singly or in groups, to a research room called a "gameroom," where they participate in "games" or other activities relevant to the development aspect being studied. Research data are collected and compared for specific groups of children—for example, three-and-a-half-year-olds and four-and-a-half-year-olds—thus protecting the privacy of each child.

Parental approval is required for all research subjects. Research supervisors preview all studies to make sure their designs and methods will yield useful information. Then the university's Human Subjects Committee and the school's research coordinator review the procedure to assure that it does not entail risk to children. Parents are given an opportunity to see the project description.

Children are allowed to participate in research between one and three hours a week, depending on the number of hours they spend at the school. Children cannot participate in research more than once a day.

Being part of a research environment is a positive experience for children at the school. They enjoy the one-to-one attention from a researcher and find the "games" stimulating.

Dissemination of Knowledge and Research to Practice

The journey from research to practice is seldom quick or easy. The reasons are many, and most are beyond the school's control. The school encourages productive dialogue between researchers and practitioners. We can assist in transferring newly generated knowledge to those for whom it was intended. At the Children's School, many early-childhood curriculum ideas are researched, developed, and implemented. Time is set aside to evaluate how children's growth and development are enhanced by the new curriculum before it is disseminated beyond the Children's School.

Funding

The university's psychology department supports the Children's School by supplying the space for the school, maintenance, and 25 percent of the director's and assistant director's salaries. The rest of the money needed for staff, curriculum supplies, and scholarships comes from tuition funds.

Grant money helps to expand the curriculum and disseminate findings and innovations; it does not support the school, which has a commitment to remain self-supporting.

History

Carnegie Mellon's Children's School is a product of many years of evolution. Until 1969 the school, then known as the Child Development Laboratory, served solely as an observation facility for students enrolled in childhood development classes in the home economics department—now defunct. Enrollment was limited to about a dozen three-year-olds, and the staff consisted of one teacher. In 1968, Dr. John Sandberg and Dr. Ann Baldwin Taylor presented a plan to the department of psychology for establishing the Children's School as a center for research into early-childhood education and the dissemination of information. They also presented a plan to nearby Chatham College for a cooperative teacher education program. With the aid of a grant from ESSO Educational Foundation in 1968, the Childhood Development Laboratory became the Children's School. The new school had a greatly expanded enrollment, a larger staff, and a new mission: to research early-childhood education, share research results with the public, and provide on-the-job experience with preschool children for undergraduate students in the new Carnegie Mellon University/Chatham College teacher education program.

The Children's School's design was partly the product of a year of studying preschools and teacher education programs in the United States and England by faculty members from Carnegie Mellon and Chatham, financed by the ESSO grant. Ideas from many sources went into planning for the school, but the most influential came from the modern English infant schools visited by faculty members during the year of study. As the number of developmental psychologists increased in the psychology department, the school sought and received more and more funding for research into children's learning.

Response

The response to the establishment of the Children's School has been gratifying. The number of applications for enrollment rises each year, and funding has increased. Parents, pleased by the school's curriculum and its philosophy of engaging families in their child's learning process, consistently recommend the school to other parents, thus playing a large role in developing the school's reputation in the Pittsburgh area. Educators and researchers from around the world visit the school to see its curriculum in action and to confer with the developmental psychologists affiliated with the school.

A Major New Cooperative Project

In 1987, the Children's School became one of twelve institutions that joined the Developmental Approaches to Science, Health, and Technology project (DASH). The DASH project offered the opportunity to join a national dissemination group and to make an impact on elementary science teaching. DASH recognizes the need to teach science interactively and to integrate it with other subject areas. It also attempts to narrow the gap between the way science is taught and the demands of a technological society. The DASH consortium works in concert to design and disseminate this new curriculum. Materials are being developed by the Curriculum Research & Development Group (CRDG) and its laboratory school at the University of Hawaii. As the project progresses, the Children's School and other consortium members are testing, adapting, and revising DASH materials. The Children's School and other consortium members are serving as demonstration sites and providing staff development workshops in the use of materials.

Since June 1988, the Buhl Foundation has provided funds to support participation by the Children's School in the DASH project. Buhl funds were awarded to cover expenses for training staff using the DASH curriculum and for follow-up support and evaluation during the school year 1988–1989. Funding was renewed in June 1989, and again in 1990, to cover staff development training and to build a support system for parents. The schools and their teachers planned fifteen workshops for parents, coordinated with the participation of fifteen classrooms in the DASH curriculum.

In 1989, with funds from Pittsburgh Cable Television, the Children's School produced a videotape to use in disseminating information about DASH to other school districts in Pennsylvania. The Children's School is also seeking funds to support DASH. Originally, two Monongahela Valley school districts took part in the DASH project; by 1989 the number had grown to twelve. About 2,250 children in the Monongahela Valley are learning from the DASH curriculum during the 1990–1991 school year. The Children's School aims to extend

DASH to all school districts in the Monongahela Valley. The school has received a grant from the National Program for Mathematics and Science (the Eisenhower program) to serve the larger urban industrialized area in the valley and beyond. The staff will produce supplementary materials, including an administrator's handbook and a family newsletter, for use throughout the area.

A LABORATORY SCHOOL
AS A CENTER FOR DEVELOPMENTAL RESEARCH

Arthur R. King, Jr.
University of Hawaii
Honolulu, Hawaii

The Present Organization, Mission, and Functions of the School

The University Laboratory School is on the main campus of the University of Hawaii. Its 340 students, ranging from kindergarten through grade 12, constitute a planned sample of the students of the state except handicapped students. Students are selected to represent the ethnic, socioeconomic, and measured I.Q. diversity of youngsters in the state. Among them are part–Hawaiian, Japanese, Caucasian, Chinese, Samoan, Filipino, Korean, Afro–American, and mixed-race children from Hawaii's multicultural population, as well as some students from Oriental and Pacific Basin cultures. Families represent professional, semiprofessional, clerical, technical, skilled, and unskilled workers, along with unemployed ones.

An essential feature of the school is its role as an integral part of the Curriculum Research & Development Group (CRDG). The Lab School, as it is commonly called, shares a common mission, site, staff, and commitment to the improvement of education through a set of related activities that include research into curriculum and instruction, design and development of curricula, teaching services to students and families, demonstrating, publishing, in-service education, and evaluation.

The school is almost completely supported by the University of Hawaii as part of its organized research program, making the CRDG/Lab School equivalent in university support to organized research units in engineering, astronomy, social science, medicine, agriculture, and other fields. Funds are appropriated by the state legislature. Minor additional funds come from the federal school lunch program and some federal funds generally available to independent schools.

The CRDG and the laboratory school are organized under the college of education. Although budget and staff are not mixed with those of the college, CRDG staff members make important contributions to the college's instructional programs by teaching undergraduate and graduate courses and supervising graduate student research. The CRDG/Lab School staff participates fully in faculty governance of the college and the university. The lab school is a "public school" in charging no tuition and in following the general mission and form of public schools. The state educational agency has no control over its program but does certify its teachers under the flexible regulations used for independent schools in the state.

The school serves as a site for idea generation and as a field base for the research and development functions of the CRDG. Daily interactions with students and families in the school context are an essential source of questions, criticisms, ideas, and hypotheses. The school also serves as the site for the first stages in the development and evaluation of programs that make up the primary output of the CRDG/Lab School. Program ideas are often developed by staff members who both teach students and serve on curriculum projects. The large, comprehensive staff numbers almost ninety.

Changes made in the school since 1966 have enabled it to assume its research and development role. Its functions have become more firmly defined into six main categories, providing

- an optimal setting for organized large-scale curriculum research, development, and evaluation.
- a stimulating environment for low-cost explorations of promising curriculum development ideas.

- a demonstration site for working curriculum models of various kinds, open to visitors from Hawaii and elsewhere.
- a site for undergraduate and graduate student research.
- a place for curriculum dialogue, teacher in-service training, seminars, and conferences.
- a quality education program for all students enrolled.

The R&D program focuses on developmental research related to the curriculum and instructional programs of the schools, along with evaluative research on school programs.

Curriculum Research—Our research encompasses the nature, problems, and possibilities of

- the school subject areas (art, drama, science, Hawaiian studies, music, marine studies, ethnic studies, English language and literature, Japanese language and culture, and mathematics, among others).
- educational topics of concern (gifted children, teacher in-service education, at-risk students, curriculum design, educational evaluation, and curriculum development in multinational settings, among others).

Curriculum Development—Our development activity has yielded a number of educational programs in wide use in this state and in several locations on the mainland United States and abroad. Among them are these:

- literature of Asian and Pacific peoples
- history of modern Hawaii
- music for elementary schools
- marine science for high schools
- composition and grammar
- language and linguistics
- computer-related education
- science for intermediate grades
- nature study for elementary schools
- nutrition for people of Hawaii and other Pacific islands
- coastal zone management
- Japanese language and culture
- science, health, and technology for elementary schools

- algebra and geometry for high schools
- ethics

The typical finished product of the curriculum research and development process consists of the following:

- a general theory of the knowledge base, including its conceptual and inquiry elements (mathematics, science, linguistics, writing, history, or other)
- a theory of instruction that accounts for various learning styles and paces of learning
- a theory of teaching
- a set of student materials
- a teacher's manual
- support materials (books, maps, reference pamphlets, activities for students, and aids to evaluation)
- a course for teacher training
- a system of publication, dissemination, and training

Record of Use—Some six hundred CRDG publications are in use. As many as 90 percent of eligible students in Hawaii use one or more of our courses. There is growing interest in some of the programs on the U.S. mainland and in several foreign countries (Japan, Australia, New Zealand, Israel, and Canada). About twelve hundred schools use Foundational Approaches in Science Teaching (FAST), the CRDG intermediate school science program.

Other Contributions—The CRDG staff is continually serving the projects, studies, and other research and school-improvement needs of the Hawaii school system. The staff is heavily involved in the academic programs of the college of education and of other colleges, serving as teachers, visiting specialists, demonstrators of instructional practice, and research advisers.

The Curriculum of the Laboratory School as an Experiment—The curriculum of the school is itself a major experiment. From kindergarten through grade 12, students participate in a common sequential curriculum and a rich program of extracurricular activities. Students are not grouped or tracked by "ability" or past performance except in the final two years of high school mathematics. One of the main purposes of this design is to eliminate in-school segregation of students and to give equal access to knowledge for all. In science, all students take a sequence of studies ending in chemistry and physics. All students enroll in three years of a foreign language—French, Japanese, or Hawaiian. All students enroll in both art and music each year, as well as physical education, social studies, and mathematics. All students are kept together in mathematics through grade 10; they have different though rigorous studies in mathematics in the eleventh and twelfth years. Full participation in extracurricular activities is urged. Over 70 percent of the boys and 60 percent of the girls participate in one or more interschool athletic programs; there is wide participation in drama.

Key Elements in the Planning/Developing Process

In the early 1960s, the three independent laboratory schools at the University of Hawaii (preschool/primary, elementary, and secondary) went through a crisis. Their traditional primary function as a site for practice teaching was considered by many to be expendable because most teachers were performing practice teaching in public schools. In addition, several externally funded experimental programs in teacher education had been conducted successfully in public schools. The students in the laboratory schools were drawn largely from faculty families and other professional and business families—a practice that undermined the school's credibility in a state committed to quality education for its lower-income, culturally different children.

The school faculties and Dean Hubert V. Everly of the college of education had committed themselves to a shift from clinical teaching practice to educational research. In 1964, Dr. David Ryans, head of the research unit of the college, solicited the views of leaders in educational research from major universities (a *Who's Who* of educational researchers of the time) on the possible roles of laboratory schools in educational research.

The issue of the schools' future was brought to a head in a formal study of their functions in 1965, conducted as a part of the extensive study of the college program. The study director was Dean Lindley J. Stiles, a respected national leader in educational research, who submitted his recommendations to the president of the university, its board of regents, and the Hawaii legislature.

The study recommended that the three schools be consolidated and that the university

> change the role and functions of the Laboratory Schools from that of demonstration and teacher training for prospective teachers to one of research and innovations [particularly of the developmental type] to improve schools and teachers in service. This action . . . is logical and needed if the Schools are to continue to justify their existence. . . . The paramount criterion should be the impact made by the Schools on the quality of education throughout the State of Hawaii. (Stiles 1966, 58–60)

The national educational agenda of the mid-1960s set the tone for the recommendation. Educational reform was part of President Johnson's "Great Society" program. The national cooperative research program had become part of the experience of university programs in education. Further, the "big project" development programs in science, mathematics, and social sciences were in full swing. The idea of university cooperation with the schools in educational improvement was encouraged.

I was appointed director of the newly consolidated school, now called the University Laboratory School. I had only recently come to Hawaii, bringing a background in teacher education, curriculum theory and design, educational administration, and cultural foundations of education. A single principal was appointed to operate the school; the director, principal, and staff, in cooperation with their colleagues from Hawaii's department of education (Hawaii has a single statewide school system) set about developing the new program focus and reshaping the school to carry it out.

The initial vision of the research role of the school was quite general, noting the promise of cooperating with the public schools and engaging in curriculum development. One desired role of the school was that of an environment for research by regular college staff, with the lab school staff providing assistance.

Then assistance appeared from an unexpected quarter. The state had received a large, continuing grant from Title III (educational innovation) of the Elementary and Secondary Education Act. It was discovered quite accidentally, at an informal coffee session after a meeting of a professional organization, that the new Title III program and the emerging laboratory school program were natural partners in school development. A Department of Education/University of Hawaii joint venture called the Hawaii Curriculum Center was started in 1966.

The new joint mission and the new resources gave a great stimulus to the emerging work agenda. The shift in efforts drew great visibility, including some tension and criticism, along with major support from the school department, the college, the state legislature, and public groups interested in education. After extensive study of the new joint organization and its programs by the legislature, the decision was made to keep the functions but to alleviate tensions by terminating the joint administration of the program, assigning control of each segment to its sponsor, the state education department or the university. The department's Title III program and the university's program were administratively separated, though considerable cooperation, including common housing, was maintained. A joint agreement approved between the two agencies in 1969 has governed the relationship for over twenty years. The university's part of the venture, including the laboratory school, became the Curriculum Research & Development Group.

Responses to the New Design

Staff—Within three years, over 80 percent of the original school staff (called "supervisors" of practice teachers under the previous model) left to take positions in the teacher education program of the college or in the public schools.

The remaining staff members were offered released time and encouraged to prepare for new roles as teacher/researchers, but only a few did. Replacements were recruited among people interested in careers in research and development. They ranged from beginning teachers to holders of doctorates.

The school had three principals before Dr. Loretta Krause, a lab school teacher with a new doctorate in educational administration, took over in 1971. She has been a major mover in developing the innovative programs of the school and its support to the R&D function. The pattern of separate staffs for school operations and R&D operations gradually gave way to a mixture of functions for all. Leaders were added for major curriculum areas and for evaluation. A new system for classifying and upgrading staff eventually yielded a staff of whom more than half enrolled in or completed doctoral programs. Staff continuity of experienced people has been remarkable.

Students in the School—After it was decided that the new functions did not require as many students, their number in the original three schools was reduced from 1,200 to 365 through attrition. Because the university continued its allocation of fifty regular faculty positions, resources were available to serve the new functions. New students were drawn to mirror the state's population. The new policy helped to validate the school's students as typifying all children in the state, and it gave the school the opportunity to experiment with changes in curricula and organizational patterns and processes for more typical students.

Constituents for the School—The changed functions also changed the constituency of the school. New, productive, and highly supportive relationships were made with

- faculty members in the arts and sciences and professional colleges of the university, who welcomed the opportunity to participate in influencing the curriculum of the school through an organized, systematic approach.
- the public school system of the state, which welcomed a partner in the school renewal program.
- policy makers on the board of education, the board of regents, the legislature, and active community groups, who saw the potential for aiding in improvement of school programs.
- schools in the university's service area, in Pacific Island territories, and, more recently, on the U.S. mainland.
- the funding source noted below.

One group of former constituents of the school was unfortunately lost: the faculty of the college of education, who regretted losing the school's commitment to teacher training and rarely identified with or participated in the new R&D programs.

Funding the Program—The fifty professional positions from the university give a stable base for the programs of the CRDG/Laboratory School. Reducing the student population made resources available for building a career staff capable of serving the combined functions of curriculum review, design, development, evaluation, dissemination, and support to schools. This basic resource has been augmented by funds from federal programs—the National Science Foundation, the National Diffusion Network, the Department of Education—and from the state's education department and other state agencies in Hawaii and elsewhere. Dissemination of CRDG programs to the U.S. mainland and elsewhere, the sale of educational materials, and provision of teacher training have extended the outreach of the CRDG.

The CRDG has a revolving account with the Research Corporation of the University of Hawaii, which handles its funds for publication and in-service training and its inventory of educational materials worth a half million dollars. We have learned that stable funding is essential to sustain an R&D program. Grants and contracts can augment but not supplant the funding base.

Unanticipated Developments and Program Modifications

Although our commitment to the improvement of schooling remains firm, our programs have continually developed and changed. We noted earlier the reduction in the number of students, the change in the composition of the student body, and the relationships established with the Hawaii Department of Education and with constituent groups and organizations. The CRDG has taken on other roles as we learned through experience what it takes to help schools change.

At first we had only a vague notion of the quantity and kinds of support required to buttress curriculum innovation—in-service training, publishing, evaluating, and networking with others in our profession. We have gained insight into the amount of care needed to support each phase in the change process and each institution joining the effort to improve curriculum. We learned to expect little from the publishing and marketing industry for small innovative curricula. We learned to avoid the host of clichés that dominate contemporary educational change. We learned to continually reinterpret our mission and to reprogram ourselves in response to our supporting university, to our other constituencies, and to political forces that can help or hinder us. We learned early why a laboratory school cannot do many functions well at the same time. Hence we do little clinical training.

Developments in the late 1970s and early 1980s have aligned the CRDG and the lab school with schools and universities in Australia, Canada, Japan, and New Zealand to improve knowledge about Pacific peoples and countries in our schools.

More recently we have established cooperative links with other laboratory schools and their supporting universities in developing and disseminating a new elementary curriculum in science, technology, and health.

Future Changes

We believe that our basic programs and approaches are sound. We will expand our set of curricula in music, art, science, math, and social studies. We are revising our secondary program in English language arts. We are investing in a larger set of strategies for educational change. For example, we are working with schools on a scheme for giving teams of teachers authority and responsibility for the school success of assigned clusters of students. The teachers plan the instructional program, monitor the progress and behavior of students, counsel them, and stay in touch with their families.

We have neglected to record and report the insights we have gained in our work; hence we will expand our writing and publishing program. We are considering boosting elementary and middle-school enrollments for projects focusing on those levels. The program in preschool education awaits better definition.

A FINAL WORD ON STRATEGIC PLANNING

Campus laboratory schools are among the less visible landmarks on the education scene. A recent writer has even referred to them as "former university laboratory schools," apparently assuming that they have slipped away into history. In fact, there are over two hundred active, productive laboratory schools in existence today. About half of them serve the elementary and secondary sectors of education; the other half are early education centers serving child-study needs of their universities. The stories of their creation and subsequent re-creation parallel the growth of education in America. These stories reveal the interplay of educational needs, the changing designs for conducting schooling, the continuing redefinition of the roles of teachers, and the changes in the curriculum. These stories also reveal strong personalities—administrators, researchers, school staffs, peers in the university, governing boards, and political constituents—who have helped their schools perfect their roles and find new niches in the changing ecology of education.

These stories of creation and renewal serve as examples of successful—and unsuccessful—strategic planning, a concept used in business, industry, universities, and increasingly in schools. Strategic planning explores factors both external and internal to an organization. Successful laboratory schools used strategic planning long before the term gained currency. Laboratory schools of the future will find that this aggressive search for the most appropriate way to direct their energies will be ever more necessary.

4

Laboratory Schools in Japan and the United States: A Comparison

Arthur R. King, Jr., and Yasushi Mizoue

UNIVERSITIES IN BOTH JAPAN AND THE UNITED STATES use elementary and secondary schools as sites for their programs of teacher training, curriculum research and development, and services to schools. Although regular public schools carry much of this load, many universities in both countries use specially formed and supported schools for these programs. Such schools are called laboratory schools in the United States and attached schools in Japan. This essay compares the roles, governance, finance, staffing, and other aspects of the two systems.

Although laboratory schools and attached schools have nearly identical functions, they evolved differently to fit the niches in the two countries. For example, the Shinonome attached elementary school, one of the oldest attached schools in Japan, was formed in 1875 to support the programs of Hiroshima Normal School. Laboratory schools appeared in the United States at about the same time and quickly became regular parts of the training programs of normal schools.

THE PLACE OF ATTACHED SCHOOLS AND LABORATORY
SCHOOLS IN EDUCATION STRUCTURES

Attached schools in Japan are standard components of its national system of higher education. Of the 96 national universities in Japan, the 56 that carry responsibility for teacher preparation support and control 260 attached schools. Of these, 48 are kindergartens, 73 are elementary schools, 78 are junior high schools, 17 are academic or vocational high schools, 42 are schools for the mentally handicapped, and one each serves blind and hearing-impaired youngsters. Hiroshima University, for example, has eleven schools, including kindergarten, elementary, junior high, and senior high schools.

Even this extensive network of attached schools cannot serve all the needs for practice teaching and other services in Japan. Many public schools cooperate with the attached schools and their associated universities. Universities not designated for teacher preparation also offer courses leading to certification. Because these universities, most of them in the private sector, have no attached schools, they use cooperating public schools for student teaching. This table summarizes the numbers of teachers trained in Japanese tertiary schools engaged in teacher preparation in 1987.

	Elementary	Junior High	Senior High
National universities in teacher education	8,977 (64%)	3,966 (43%)	1,099 (14%)
Other universities (national, public, and private)	3,821 (27%)	4,564 (50%)	5,915 (76%)
Junior colleges	994 (7%)	398 (4%)	19 (.2%)
Graduate courses	146 (1%)	202 (2%)	756 (10%)
TOTAL	13,938	9,130	7,789

National universities with major teacher education programs prepare most of the elementary school teachers, under half of the junior high school teachers, and a minority of the high school teachers of the country.

Laboratory schools in the United States are not part of a national system. Each one is formed, shaped, and resourced within its host university to serve locally determined functions. This decentralization parallels that of the systems of state and local control of both higher education and the schools.

Laboratory schools are of two kinds. About a hundred serve teacher preparation programs for their sponsoring universities. These schools have banded together in the National Association of Laboratory Schools. Another hundred are centers for early education, largely for children of preschool age, that serve as laboratories for studying child growth and development but do not lead to careers in teaching. The National Organization of Child Development Laboratory Schools represents this group. This essay treats only the first group, the schools analogous to Japanese attached schools. In contrast to Japan, few of the older public universities in the United States maintain laboratory schools. Most are maintained by younger universities with major commitments to teacher education.

American laboratory schools are typically on university campuses. They vary in age/grade levels served. The greatest number are early education and elementary schools; fewer are junior high or middle schools; still fewer are high schools. No laboratory schools specialize in vocational education. It follows that most teacher education students receive their practice teaching and other clinical experiences in regular public schools.

MISSION OF ATTACHED SCHOOLS AND LABORATORY SCHOOLS

The attached schools of Japan operate primarily as sites for practice teaching. They also serve teachers in training as observation sites; they serve professionals as demonstration sites; they support research and publication by university faculty members; they offer consultation to schools on request. Teachers in attached schools may assist in writing textbooks and instructional materials for commercial publishers; sometimes they serve public schools as lecturers; often they teach part-time in universities.

Because staff members of attached schools are familiar with school practice, they are valuable to schools of education, counterbalancing the theoretic bent of most professors of education.

American laboratory schools present a more varied picture. The following table shows the functions considered most important by sixty-two laboratory schools reporting in the survey begun in 1987 by the National Association of Laboratory Schools (Johnson 1987).

Number of Schools Ranking Each Function First

Function	Number
Clinical teaching experiences	25
Curriculum development	10
Observation	7
Research	5
Staff development	4
Demonstration	3
Experimentation	2
Student teaching	2
Other	4

The terms in the table need defining because they are not used in consistent senses in laboratory schools and schools of education. (This ambiguity in language demonstrates two characteristics of American education today: changing programs reflected in changes in terminology, and the autonomy of schools of education, including their laboratory schools, within flexible national standards.)

1. *Clinical teaching experience* refers to observation and participation in the activities of a class with less responsibility than during

the practice-teaching period later in the program. Clinical experience is recommended throughout the full teacher-training course.

2. *Curriculum development* refers to the design, crafting, and experimental use of curricula and supporting materials different from those used in most schools. A curriculum may be used only in the school for observation by college students and teachers from the local schools, or it may be published and disseminated regionally, nationally, or even internationally.

3. *Observation* means occasional visits to a laboratory school to watch a particular lesson or teaching practice.

4. *Demonstration* is usually an arranged presentation of a lesson or educational practice, not necessarily distinguished from observation.

5. *Research* can mean any number of kinds of investigations directed either by professors in the university or by the laboratory school staff itself.

6. *Staff development,* a fast-growing function, refers to formal training activities for teachers in local schools.

7. *Experimentation* can mean any of a number of preliminary innovations less systematic or less sustained than research or curriculum development.

8. *Student teaching,* as in Japan, refers to the period when a prospective teacher takes rather complete control of a class under the supervision of the teacher and the college instructor. The period of practice teaching is usually longer in the United States than in Japan.

Practice teaching, the prime function of attached schools in Japan, is the major function in only a few American schools. The survey also reported functions not listed in the table—"leading edge" functions in laboratory school practice, including graduate practical programs, internships, and graduate assistant programs. The increased attention to research, development, and experimentation and to staff development for local schools is the most striking recent change.

ORGANIZATION AND ADMINISTRATION OF ATTACHED SCHOOLS AND LABORATORY SCHOOLS

The attached schools of Japan are established and financed by the Mombusho, the national ministry of education, which sets the budget and allocates teaching positions by a formula for school size and function.

In each Japanese university a set of committees establishes policies and procedures and guides the development and operation of its attached schools. Under the overall committee, other committees of university faculty and school staff members are assigned to study and manage such functions as student teaching, the setting of bylaws, co-operative study between university faculty and school staff, and selecting students from among the applicants to the attached schools.

The attached schools have the initiative to plan the school curriculum without assistance from the university faculty. But because of the centralizing tendencies of the Japanese national education system, curriculum content and organization, class size, instructional equipment, teaching practices, and other school features are quite similar to those in other Japanese schools. Attached schools have traditionally been near university campuses, but newer ones are often some distance away.

Laboratory schools in the United States present a great variety of patterns of organization and control. Typically the schools are organized as sections of a college- or university-based school (or department) of education or teacher education. Deans of colleges (or chairs of departments) of education, college faculties, laboratory school administrators, and school staffs are common members of the controlling structures. In some cases state legislators and officials, university presidents and budgetmakers, and local school authorities, because they hold the power of the purse strings, exert some influence over the form, function, size, resources—and even the survival—of laboratory schools. Because colleges and departments within universities must constantly compete for resources, the leaders and constituents of laboratory schools must constantly attend to their connections with politically important people in the university and in government.

Patterns of fiscal support for laboratory schools differ. Funds can come from the sponsoring university's budget for teacher education, from the university's research budget, from the state or local school district for per pupil expenditure (often a "flow-through" from the state), from local tax revenues, from federal or state grants, and from gifts. Some schools attached to private universities also collect tuition and fees. Two laboratory schools for the deaf are fully supported by the national government.

STAFFS OF ATTACHED SCHOOLS AND LABORATORY SCHOOLS

Japanese attached schools typically recruit experienced teachers from the public schools. The school principal selects the teachers; the president of the university approves the appointments. Service in attached schools is seen as career-enhancing, and the prestige of affiliation with such a school compensates for the drop in salary that comes with the transfer. Most attached-school teachers wish to continue educational study, but they are rarely accorded sabbatical leaves or opportunities to take courses or earn advanced degrees. They are usually encouraged to return to public schools in mid-career, and most do. Some are promoted to supervisory positions in local boards of education; others take positions in the university, where they remain as regular, permanent members of the staff.

The primary duties of attached-school teachers are to teach the elementary and secondary students in their classes and to provide practice-teaching environments for teachers in training. They often produce teaching resources to meet the interests and maturity levels of their students. Their wider professional activities were noted under the mission of the schools.

Laboratory school staffs in the United States have similar characteristics and follow similar career paths, but there is great variation among schools. Many of their teachers move on to careers in public schools after a few years. Those who stay beyond six or seven years tend to make permanent careers in laboratory schools. In years past it was common for laboratory school teachers to move into positions in their universities; now it happens only rarely. Teachers are encouraged—often offered opportunities—to undertake advanced study. Beyond their teaching duties, the professional activities of these teachers reflect the schools' diverse missions cited earlier.

In laboratory schools with links to local school districts, mixed patterns of appointment and certification are common. Sometimes teachers are appointed by the cooperating school district; sometimes the university has some voice in appointments to and continued service in the schools. No studies are available on compensation, but salaries are thought to be well below those of local public schools.

STUDENTS IN ATTACHED SCHOOLS AND LABORATORY SCHOOLS

Students in attached schools in Japan are drawn from the residential area served by the schools. The schools make no special effort to assure that their populations resemble those of the area's public schools. All students may apply, and children of faculty members in the school or the university receive no special consideration. Neither the gender of the child nor the income of the parents figures in admission. At the primary level a skills test and an interview are part of the screening process, with selection from the qualifying group made by random drawing. Admission to high schools is based on high examination scores. Graduation from an attached school is believed to improve a student's chances of admission to prestigious universities.

In American laboratory schools the composition of the student body depends on the school's mission. The laboratory school at the University of Hawaii, for example, specializes in research and development of the curriculum, so it selects a planned sample of the children of the state by ethnicity, gender, socioeconomic status of parents, and learning rate as estimated by test scores. Other laboratory schools give preferred admission to handicapped or gifted children, children from faculty families, or tuition-paying families. As in Japan, laboratory schools are usually seen as an avenue to long-term educational success, including admission to selective universities.

ISSUES AND CONCERNS

These specialized schools in both Japan and the United States must be viewed in their national educational context. Both nations are concerned with the performance of schools and of teachers, especially new ones. Both nations see improvement in teacher education programs as essential to solving problems in schooling.

Because Japanese leaders in education are not satisfied with the performance of new teachers, local education boards require intensive in-service training during the first years. Attached schools now have no role in in-service training of beginning teachers, but some U.S. laboratory schools are finding this an area of important service.

Japanese attached schools are overburdened with practice teachers. The Shinonome attached school, for example, has ten student teachers to a single class. Japanese national standards require five weeks of practice teaching for the elementary certificate, three weeks for the junior and senior high school certificate. Some universities, finding the requirements inadequate, require more. Hiroshima University, for example, requires seven weeks for elementary candidates, five for secondary candidates.

In Japan there is increasing demand for more collaboration between attached schools and universities in teacher education and educational research. At Hiroshima University the education faculty and faculty from other divisions join the staff of the attached school for joint study of student teaching. Faculty members attend the annual conference of attached schools to offer comment. To reciprocate, school staff members are invited to attend university classes to demonstrate teaching strategies and techniques. Finally, the new Japanese course of study requires collaboration in developing new methods of teaching.

In the United States both general schooling and teacher education are under fire from the profession, state and national governments, and the public. As an example, the Holmes Group, representing about a hundred major universities, is calling for reform in teacher education. Among other changes, it is proposing "professional development schools"—publicly operated schools devoted to teacher education, research, development, and innovation. Leaders in the Holmes Group do not consider university-based laboratory schools right for this effort. But laboratory school people disagree, maintaining that a university base is essential to shaping and supporting dynamic and credible programs of pre-service and in-service education as well as programs of research, development, and innovation. Advocates of laboratory schools believe their record of success proves them credible as special-mission agencies when they are properly led and supported.

A comparison of the university-operated lower schools of the two nations reveals striking similarities as well as some differences. We see reflected in these schools the difference between the centralized national educational system of Japan and the decentralized educational systems of the United States. We see more variety and flexibility in the decentralized system but find value and appeal in a well-resourced national system. The specialized university-supported schools reflect the educational visions and needs of the two countries, amazingly common in the light of historical and cultural differences.

5

Governance and Financing of Laboratory Schools

Crayton L. Buck and Jackson J. Martin

SHARED GOVERNANCE IN LABORATORY SCHOOLS

COLLEGES AND UNIVERSITIES HAVE A LONG TRADITION of shared governance. Shared governance means interaction of faculty and administration in making decisions to benefit the institution and its programs. To share in governance, faculty members must participate in policy making, peer review, faculty selection, program planning, and curriculum development and review. Though governance practices vary among institutions, commitment to the process varies little. Members may disagree about the type and degree of participation, but not about the concept.

Shared governance requires clear definition of the locus of the authority to set and administer policy. Governance is based on certain clear-cut ideas, confidence in reason and fairness, faith in cooperative rather than adversarial interactions, and collaboration in implementing decisions. When faculty from different fields meet with administrators to analyze and discuss issues, the outcomes are usually more realistic and more workable than they are when either group reaches independent conclusions.

Over the past twenty-five years collective bargaining has affected the governance process. Although relationships have sometimes been adversarial, the bargaining procedure is better viewed as another means of protecting and strengthening shared governance by clarifying issues, assuring faculty participation, defining processes, ensuring communication, and avoiding domination by policy makers and enforcers. Everyone is better served because the bilateral approach brings better results in information, understanding, compromise, and respect.

Laboratory schools, by virtue of their association with institutions of higher education, participate in the shared governance process. This feature usually sets them apart from schools operated by public boards of education. Shared governance is an aspiration for public schools; it is a reality in university-based laboratory schools.

Shared governance raises fundamental questions for a laboratory school: Who controls the destiny of the school? What is its relationship to other college or university departments? What part does it play in faculty governance? What is the status of laboratory school personnel vis-à-vis faculty rank, promotion, tenure, and remuneration? What criteria are laboratory school personnel expected to meet for appointment and reappointment? All these questions are critical to the manner in which laboratory school teachers perceive themselves, as well as how others in the higher education community view them. Perceptions of self relate directly to the performance of tasks.

Laboratory schools are usually able to operate with considerable administrative freedom. Although a few have advisory boards, most have administrators who are directly responsible to a dean, vice-president, or provost. Thus they are a part of the structure that makes decisions and sets policies. Many laboratory school administrators are also considered managerial staff, hence not part of a negotiating unit. This position gives leaders of laboratory schools an important role in the governance structure. Representing laboratory school interests is only one part of their role because they also interact with other departmental leaders. The astute administrator, by using the governance system to develop linkages with other sections in the university, increases the likelihood of broadly based support for the school.

FINANCING LABORATORY SCHOOLS

Achieving two or more sets of purposes in one school can be costly. If educating children were the sole purpose, the expense of operating laboratory schools in universities could be prohibitive. However, when all the functions performed by laboratory schools in teacher education and related educational programs are taken into account, the schools are cost-effective, perhaps among the best bargains in the profession.

Funds to support laboratory schools come from both public and private sectors. Public funds are allocated by federal, state, or local governmental jurisdictions. Private funds, on the other hand, come from foundations, from the institution of higher education, or from direct levies on the clientele served—that is, tuition. Because some public institutions cannot charge tuition, they sometimes levy admission fees, instructional fees, activity fees, laboratory fees, or fees for textbook and equipment rental. The financial base of a laboratory school may be a combination of public and private monies. However, no pattern is discernible because local decisions affect funding mixes.

Fifty schools in public universities and twelve in private universities reported their sources of income in a 1987 survey conducted by the National Association of Laboratory Schools (Johnson 1987). The typical school draws funds from three sources. All schools in private universities charge tuition, and most draw funds also from their college or university. The survey did not yield data on the amounts of funds from each source or the mix of funds coming to any one school.

Laboratory School Funding Sources

	Public Lab Schools	Private Lab Schools
	N = 50	N = 12
State funds	34	1
Local school agency	13	0
College or university	30	9
Tuition	15	12
Fees	20	4
Contracts	7	1
Grants	16	3
Other	5	0

Public College and University Budgets

Funds for laboratory schools connected with public universities are typically built into the instructional budget of the college of education. Institutional support comes not only in direct allotments of funds and positions but in other forms such as space, utilities, and services. In the case of the laboratory school at the University of Hawaii, funds come from the university's institutional research budget, just as they do for research institutes in astronomy, agriculture, or medicine.

These determinations reflect the primary mission of the school, be it teacher education or research and development. For support in the university's budget, laboratory schools must make their justification to the hierarchy that determines university funding, typically including university colleagues, college and university administrators, governing boards, state budget authorities, governors, and, ultimately, legislatures. Because this lengthy process provides many points of review, laboratory school administrators and their constituents must work constantly at sustaining or improving their schools' reputation to assure steady funding.

Contractual Arrangements with Local School Districts

Contracts or agreements between institutions of higher education and one or more school districts are emerging as ways of financing laboratory schools.

Such agreements meet the needs of both cooperating parties. Colleges of education are interested primarily in preparing their students to become teachers or to enter graduate school; school districts are interested primarily in educating children.

Cooperative agreements with school districts must be negotiated carefully, especially in states where teachers are organized for collective bargaining. Contract conditions are a negotiable matter, but participation in a teacher preparation program is voluntary and therefore not negotiable. Negotiating a cooperative agreement can be further complicated when more than one bargaining unit is involved. When colleges or universities enter into negotiations, they must have a carefully designed plan of action, and they must know their positions on the following issues:

- definition of the employer
- process for selecting the administrator/coordinator
- job description for the administrator/coordinator
- criteria for selecting participating faculty
- job descriptions for participating faculty
- process for evaluating participating teachers
- composition of any advisory committee
- policy responsibilities of advisory committees
- manner in which prospective teachers participate in programs
- procedures for resolving conflicts surfacing from any source

One of the more unusual collaborations is the one supported by New York's State University College at Buffalo and the City of Buffalo. In 1977 the College Learning Laboratory was committed to assisting in the city's desegregation plan by becoming a magnet school. (The assignment also helped the college meet accreditation requirements in multicultural, special, and urban education.) The school remains a laboratory school in that it provides clinical teaching experiences and conducts research. About a quarter of the students have a physical, mental, or learning impairment—areas where research is needed.

The Buffalo model is important because it highlights the challenges of merging disparate elements under one roof. The college and the city each contribute half of the teaching faculty and operating funds. The college provides the facility and maintenance services. Altogether, nearly eight hundred students and eighty professionals work together to provide educational programs for children and prospective teachers.

Indiana State University operates its laboratory school in accordance with an agreement with its county school corporation (school district), which assigns students to the school. The county corporation counts these students in its membership and forwards funds allocated by the state education department to the university for the students in the laboratory school. This agreement is made under Indiana Public Law 99, 1974, which states that agreements

> may be entered into with local school units and educational organizations for the assignment of pupils to such laboratory schools, the payment of transfer fees, and contributions to the cost of establishing and maintaining said schools.

In this pattern, state funds are generally referred to as "flow-through funds." The pattern allows state aid originally allotted to local school districts to be used for students enrolled in laboratory schools. It also provides a funding formula that is fair to the school district where the laboratory school is located. Since the basic state allocation covers only part of the cost of schooling for students, the college or university must supplement it to meet the total cost of operation. This university support is analogous to allocations from local property taxes that supplement state allocations. The money from the college or university covers the cost of services it performs in teacher preparation and related college programs.

Several states, including Florida, Illinois, Kentucky, Louisiana, Oregon, and Tennessee, use this approach, but details differ, even within a state. For example, some Louisiana schools receive operating funds directly through the university budget, while others are funded through agreements with the local parish (school district) under the flow-through method. Florida, on the other hand, channels funds to the university budget on the basis of full-time equivalents. This base allocation is supplemented by the county.

Laboratory schools at Illinois State University receive money from the several school districts from which their students are drawn. Funds from each school district are calculated according to the number of students enrolled in the laboratory school. Since there are several participating school districts, state aid follows the formula of each district. Thus more money per pupil may come from one school district than from another.

Illinois State University also receives school district aid for children in special education. Its two laboratory schools—Metcalf Elementary and University High—have large programs of special education. Funding for special students comes through contractual service agreements by whose terms the contracting agency pays the university at the same rate it pays other school districts.

The formulas in these flow-through patterns are developed to meet the needs of the institution and the state. Furthermore, they achieve an equity in funding that makes for a better working relationship with the public schools.

Public Laboratory Schools as Separate School Districts

Indiana provides for the state's education department to establish laboratory schools as separate school districts. Public Law 99, 1974, permits Indiana University, Purdue University, Indiana State University, and Ball State University to establish and conduct laboratory schools at their main campuses. The law specifies the purpose of such schools and allows for constructing and equipping buildings for them. The law also specifies the nature of funding and the kinds of arrangements that may be made with local school units, if any.

Ball State chooses to have no agreement with local school units; it is a separate school district of the state. In theory, any resident of Indiana is eligible to attend the Burris Laboratory School at Ball State. Under this arrangement, the 1974 Public Law 99 provides a funding formula:

A university which operates a laboratory school under this chapter without an agreement with a local school unit or an educational organization shall receive all the state financial assistance that the largest school corporation in the county in which the university is located would have received per pupil.

The local school corporation (school district) of residence is not permitted to count pupils in the Burris Laboratory School as part of its enrollment.

Federal Funding for Laboratory Schools

The laboratory schools at Gallaudet College—Kendall Demonstration Elementary School and the Model Secondary School for the Deaf—are the only laboratory schools funded wholly by the federal government. They not only develop and demonstrate the best current practices for educating hearing-impaired students; they also conduct research and development of technologies for impairments of hearing and speech. Students attending Gallaudet College who plan a career in teaching hearing-impaired students go to these schools for their clinical teaching experiences.

The Kendall School, a day school, serves primarily the District of Columbia and nearby school districts in Maryland and Virginia. The Model Secondary School, a residential school, selects its students from hearing-impaired applicants of secondary school age in the United States or its territories. No tuition is charged at either school.

Many laboratory schools receive indirect federal funds under the child-benefit decisions of the U.S. Supreme Court. These funds support such services to students as transportation, school lunch, counseling, and other benefits for low-income students and other special clienteles. Though limited, these funds are important because regular financial sources typically do not cover those services.

Financing Laboratory Schools in Private Colleges and Universities

Private colleges and universities operating laboratory schools do not offer free (or nearly free) schooling. These schools must charge hefty tuitions—sometimes even the full cost. Like schools in public higher institutions, private schools provide services for teacher preparation programs in a variety of disciplines. Often, though, the private laboratory schools, in response to the desires of tuition-paying parents, tend to emphasize education for children rather than service to academic and professional programs. Among the exceptions is the Baker Demonstration School of the National College of Education. This college maintains its original focus as a single-purpose institution for preparing teachers and administrators. Though the Baker School is tuition-driven, it is committed to the college's teacher-preparation mission.

Laboratory schools associated with religious denominations have the additional function of inculcating beliefs associated with their religious philosophies.

The tuition for private laboratory schools is used for the direct costs of teaching students. The college usually supports the school by maintaining its plant and grounds and covering the costs of light and heat.

Although private laboratory schools are eligible for federal and state funds, they are not required to seek or accept them. But when they do, they must comply with guidelines regulating their use. Local school districts that have private schools, including laboratory schools, in their jurisdictions must offer them the opportunity to participate in federally funded programs. If a school decides to participate, the school district must follow procedures to account for the use of funds. School districts are also required to provide services such as busing, library books, and textbooks under the child-benefit ruling of the Supreme Court. These services have been helpful in enhancing many laboratory school programs.

CONCLUSION

Governance of laboratory schools may be characterized as unique in the educational community because of the university tradition of shared governance. The mesh within the larger operation of the college or university is critical because it requires the schools' leaders to demonstrate the worth of their schools.

Finances are always a critical issue in education, and when budgets are tight or recession looms, laboratory schools are attractive targets. Hence it is essential that they have a solid financial base and parent institutions that foster a supportive political climate. Searching for funds and allocating them prudently will continue to be important tasks for laboratory schools.

6

Showcasing Laboratory Schools

This chapter describes the programs of thirty laboratory schools that responded to the editor's invitation to send profiles. The schools are listed alphabetically by state. Some entries had to be pared in the cause of economy. Readers wanting to know more can find the schools' addresses in a directory in the Appendix. The chapter was organized by Kate D'Erasmo and Peg Forrester of the College Learning Laboratory and Loretta Krause of the University of Hawaii Laboratory School.

ALABAMA

Teaching Learning Center
Jacksonville State University
Jacksonville, Alabama

The Teaching Learning Center is a tuition-free campus school for students from kindergarten through grade 12. Students are accepted through direct application. As a unit of the university, the center provides clinical experiences required in the teacher education program of the college of education. Tutoring skills are emphasized, and teachers in training learn practical skills in classroom techniques.

The center was established in 1982 to provide pre-service students of the college with supervised instruction and practical experience. On completing their practical courses, the students will have acquired some teaching experience, learned how to use current educational materials, reviewed videotapes of their activities, and familiarized themselves with methods of teaching that are effective with children of differing ages and ability levels.

Laboratory Nursery School
Jacksonville State University
Jacksonville, Alabama

The Laboratory Nursery School supports the instructional goals of the university by providing college students and faculty members with opportunities for study and research in early childhood education. Tuition is $115 a semester for children enrolled in the nursery school.

The goals of the school are to offer university students opportunities to work with children in the school setting and to provide the children with an environment that will foster optimum development in all areas of their lives.

The school's philosophy recognizes that each child is unique and develops at his or her own rate. This philosophy has yielded a program designed to promote social, physical, emotional, and mental development. Among the goals that assist each child in maturation are growing in independence, learning to develop self-control, learning to function with other children, learning to develop large and small motor skills, developing a higher level of mental functioning (reasoning and making associations, for example), and developing self-confidence.

CALIFORNIA

Seeds University Elementary School
University of California, Los Angeles
Los Angeles, California

This school is described in Chapter 3.

FLORIDA

Henderson University School
Florida Atlantic University
Boca Raton, Florida

The Alexander D. Henderson University School opened in 1968 on the campus of Florida Atlantic University, a state-supported university that had opened ten years earlier. A private donation by the widow of Alexander D. Henderson provided funds for constructing and furnishing the school and established a trust fund to ensure a margin of excellence for its programs.

Henderson, which enrolls children from kindergarten through grade 8, is classified as a special-purpose public school. It operates as a demonstration site for teacher education, conducts research, and develops curricula. Except for a minimal annual activities fee, funding for the school's operation comes from the state. Attendance is voluntary, and students from two counties, Broward and Palm Beach, are eligible to apply for admission.

As a demonstration site, the school is a partner of the university in teacher education. It is an ideal setting for observing current instructional styles and strategies. It is the required location for pre–student-teaching experiences of undergraduates in the college, who come to watch demonstrations ranging from general classroom activities to the presentation of specific subject matter to groups of pupils. Outstanding teacher candidates are invited to complete their student-teaching experience at the school. Service to schools and to practicing teachers in surrounding counties is offered through the Teacher Education Center, professional visitations, workshops, demonstration tapes, and related activities.

Physical education and selected areas in the humanities are part of ongoing curriculum development at the school. This curriculum emphasizes mastery of basic skills in all areas. Enrichment activities in the subject areas expand the basic curriculum to challenge and motivate students.

As a research site, the school generates its own teacher-directed research, thereby serving the college of education, other colleges and departments in the university, the community, and private industry.

University School of Nova University
Nova University
Fort Lauderdale, Florida

The University School of Nova stresses the development of positive self-image along with sound academics. The school teaches responsibility and decision-making along with a strict academic curriculum. Advanced curriculum in small classes meets the needs of students ranging from average to gifted. Minimal stress and competition allow children to learn comfortably, while their academic achievement challenges that of any school.

Individualized instruction lights children's faces at this school. No child is ever held to a given grade level. Children are allowed to learn as rapidly as they can, mastering skills appropriate to their ability, often while crossing grade levels.

From pre-kindergarten four-year-olds to eighth-graders in honors math, computer-assisted instruction and computer programming equip students with skills and attitudes for tomorrow's technology. Uniquely characteristic of the school are tailored electives for grades 6 through 8 which grow out of the staff's knowledge of each child's ability and learning style.

A primary goal of the staff is to provide a dynamic, exciting, and challenging learning environment for all students by presenting a blend of gifted programming activities throughout the total program. Studies now indicate that it is not enough to have a gifted program that "pulls out" students for a few hours a week with a single coordinator. A "gifted program" should be "gifted education," with the responsibility in the hands of everyone associated with a child's development. Gifted services offered throughout the school day give all children the opportunity to develop their unique talents and potentials, tapping the capabilities of gifted students and students not identified as gifted. These able students have worthwhile talents and strengths that may have been overlooked but need nurturing.

GEORGIA

Berry College Laboratory School
Berry College
Mount Berry, Georgia

The Berry College Laboratory School, originally called the Early Learning Center, was founded in 1977 as a demonstration center following the philosophy of British infant schools. Funded originally by the Lilly Foundation, the school serves Berry College's departments of education and psychology in preparing teachers. It also serves the college's Work Opportunity Program by employing college students as instructional aides, bus drivers, kitchen assistants, and teachers in special subject areas. Student tuition is supplemented by support from Berry College to finance the school.

Berry's 28,000-acre home on the outskirts of Rome, Georgia, is the largest college campus in the world. Lab school children travel a three-mile country road, passing ponds, a lake, woods, and wild animals on their way to the lab school's mountain campus. Outdoor adventures and nature study are important features of the school day. The metropolitan Atlanta area, sixty-five miles southeast of Rome, offers a valuable contrast to the rural setting, and children often go there for museum or theater outings.

About a hundred children from a sixty-mile radius are served in kindergarten through grade 5. The school seeks diversity in its student body, and a small minority-incentive grant is available. Children of professional and nonprofessional parents are about evenly balanced. Most children live in two-parent homes, with both parents employed outside the home. About 10 percent of the students have been identified as having special needs.

In a nurturing, family-like environment, children learn by doing, by cooperating, by peer teaching, and by solving real-life problems. Students in grades 3 through 5 are cross-grade grouped in "base communities," where they study written composition, art, physical education, French, and music. Kindergartners and first- and second-graders are grouped by grade for these subjects.

Language arts and mathematics are taught in achievement groupings. Children from three or four grades may be working together in math or reading. Reading instruction, which follows the whole-language orientation, is conducted primarily through the use of child-authored materials, children's literature, and content materials. Math is taught in an enriched environment planned for sensory-motor learning. Through developmentally appropriate concrete experiences, children reinvent basic principles from mathematics, science, and social studies.

The composition program follows a writing-as-process model. Writing comes first in the school day to highlight its importance. Pictographs and letter-name and letter-sound spellings are used by early writers. Mature writers grow in their use of writing conventions as they revise, edit, and share their work.

College students in their junior year come to the school two hours a week for course-related practicum experiences. Some of them are also sent to the school to observe or work in conjunction with coursework during the other years of the program. Demonstration lessons, pre-teaching briefings, and discussions following the lessons are conducted by lab school teachers for college classes on request of the college faculty. The school also serves as a site for educational research conducted by Berry College faculty.

Teachers with diverse life experiences have been recruited by the school to enrich the curriculum. Four of the five full-time teachers hold master's degrees; the fifth teacher is finishing this degree. Commitment to a child-centered, child-initiated, sensory-motor approach to learning is a prerequisite to success in teaching at the lab school.

Parents also enrich the school as instructional aides, teachers of special workshops, and leaders in development activities in the community. Parent-teacher communication is fostered through narrative written reports and parent conferences three times a year. Informal communication is encouraged through frequent phone calls and notes.

HAWAII

University Laboratory School
University of Hawaii
Honolulu, Hawaii

This school is described in the latter part of Chapter 3.

ILLINOIS

Baker Demonstration School
National College of Education
Evanston, Illinois

The original demonstration school opened in the fall of 1918, but its roots go back to the founding of the college in 1886. Elizabeth Harrison, its founder, worked with Jane Addams, founder of Hull House. The school flourished. By the 1920s, faculty members had taken up John Dewey's philosophy of educating the whole child. A child's total development needs—emotional, physical, and social as well as intellectual—are individually considered at the Baker Demonstration School. Academic work proceeds within a learning framework designed to insure that students master many skills. Projects such as writing stories, producing plays, compiling books of their own stories, and shooting films make learning exciting as well as effective for students.

Baker teachers teach concepts and computations by using concrete, manipulative materials, then building new knowledge on foundations children already have. Beyond maintaining skills through practice, teachers arrange opportunities for students to apply their acquired skills in solving practical problems. Guided by their knowledge of students' developmental levels and personal abilities, teachers decide on the balance of time and emphasis to give each area of instruction. The transfer of knowledge from one situation to a new one is enhanced by following an integrated curriculum.

The curriculum is broad-based, with arts emphasized along with the content areas. Foreign language is available for children from age three because exposure to a language in the early years lets children hear, sing, and play in the language before they begin a formal program. Other curricular areas, from computer learning to swimming, offer experiences in academic and nonacademic areas.

Most instruction during a school year emphasizes a theme woven through the curriculum. Special programs, as well as a visiting artist series, bring the theme alive in different ways. The arts are used as a means of integrating the theme into the curriculum. A school fair or an all-school show that includes song, drama, and movement lets children share what they learned with other children in the school.

University High School
University of Illinois at Urbana–Champaign
Urbana, Illinois

University High School is a teaching, research, and service unit of the University of Illinois at Urbana–Champaign. As a laboratory, the school is a resource to local, regional, state, and national educational communities. As an accredited high school, it offers a five-year, fast-paced educational program for academically talented college-bound students. Its educational mission is characterized by three hallmarks: high academic standards, experimentation and innovation, and demonstration of excellence in teaching. Faculty members are master teachers who demonstrate effective teaching for high academic attainment.

This school is a center for translating educational research and theory into practice and for systematic field-testing of applications. Expert practitioners, educational researchers, and junior high and high school students create a dynamic environment where ideas are freely exchanged in a real-school setting. The process of translating theory and research into practice yields new or revised curricula, text materials, improved teaching and instructional practices or programs, innovative approaches to teacher training, advanced educational technologies, and more efficient forms of organizing and managing a school. Once theory is translated into effective practices, the school helps to disseminate these practices.

The school offers an educational program for academically gifted students of any race, creed, or economic background. It tries to create a climate where students with common concerns, abilities, and interests can form satisfying social relationships. Most important, the school program challenges gifted and talented students to put forth their best efforts. Its curriculum stresses critical and flexible thinking, the value of lifelong learning, and tolerance for varied points of view and cultural values.

Social advocacy, an interdisciplinary social studies/English program, is designed to educate students for citizenship, to introduce them to the community, to involve them as volunteers in social agencies, to enhance their learning through field experiences, and to form a partnership between the school and the community. Students examine the history of social problems and treatments, from the poorhouse to the welfare system, from the decline of the American family to the support groups and agencies that try to sustain it.

The course offers an innovative approach to learning through exchanging ideas, insights, and experiences and being open to new information and perspectives. Students rehearse communication and group dynamics in social agencies such as a nursing home, a day-care center, a literacy classroom, a group home for retarded adults, or an after-school tutoring program for minority children—experiences that bring them face to face with struggling people and connect the theory of the classroom with the reality of the world. The social advocacy course fosters the awareness and responsibility that citizens need for meeting the challenges of an ever-changing society.

At the school is the National Center for the Teaching of Japanese Language and Culture in High School, which develops language and culture materials for high schools. The center conducts surveys and offers regional workshops for Japanese language teachers, and it coordinates a network of over three hundred high school teachers of Japanese and issues a quarterly newsletter to members of this network.

The National Center for School Leadership is an R&D center funded by $2.5 million of federal funds for five years, 1988–1993. This award to a laboratory school is a landmark—the first such award ever made to a laboratory school. Although laboratory schools have long experimented and innovated, large federal grants have typically been beyond their reach since the early 1960s because much of the money has gone into R&D centers and regional educational laboratories.

The National Center for School Leadership has three broad objectives:

- to produce new knowledge about school leadership, especially as it relates to facilitating teaching and learning
- to design training programs and materials for improving school leadership
- to influence the training of school leaders and their practice of leadership through local, state, and national policy formation, collaborative exchanges, and dissemination of information

The school serves as a case study of the effects of school leadership and shared governance on site-based management. New leadership practices, along with methods of studying and improving leadership, are field-tested in the school, making it a source of new ideas for effective school leadership.

INDIANA

Burris Laboratory School
Ball State University
Muncie, Indiana

Burris Laboratory School has been an integral part of the teacher education program at Ball State University since the school opened in 1929. In 1974 the Indiana General Assembly passed a law giving the university the right to operate its laboratory school as an independent school district. When the Burris–Ball State School Corporation was created, Burris became a school district without boundaries, having authority to enroll any student living in Indiana.

Students apply for admission. The admission committee is charged with maintaining roughly equal numbers of boys and girls, a balance of socioeconomic and ability levels, and a student body that reflects the proportions of minorities in the population and schools of Muncie–Delaware County. Within recent years the school has had three to four applicants for each opening.

Burris operates as three schools within one building—a grade K–5 elementary school, a grade 6–8 middle school, and a grade 9–12 high school.

The elementary school and the middle school have two sections per grade; the high school averages about seventy students per grade. There are about 290 students in the elementary school, 180 in the middle school, and 280 in the high school. There is also a pull-out program for about sixty students with learning disabilities and speech or hearing problems.

Burris's primary function has been to provide pre–practice-teaching clinical experiences for students in the university's teacher education programs. Some clinical experiences are scheduled in public schools within traveling distance of the university, but Burris continues to provide a large share of these experiences, especially for majors in elementary education. The university does not use Burris for student-teaching assignments.

Departments and colleges throughout the university use Burris for clinical experiences. During a single year more than 25,000 hours of clinical experiences were conducted at Burris. Students used Burris to meet requirements for more than thirty-five courses, many of which had multiple sections. Every student enrolled at Burris and every teacher has multiple contacts with college students working in some way in the Burris program.

In 1988 the Indiana General Assembly gave Ball State University the right to establish a statewide residential academy for three hundred gifted students in grades 11 and 12. This academy opened in September 1990. The academy is not a part of Burris Laboratory School, but it is being housed in the Burris building. To accommodate the academy, Burris is reducing its enrollment from 750 to 450. It will maintain a K–12 program, but a cutback in resources requires some curricular restructuring.

Ball State University has made a strong commitment to use Burris as a part of its interactive television program. A state-of-the-art telecommunications building was opened on campus in 1988, and plans are being formulated to broadcast programs via satellite throughout the state. In 1988–1989, Burris used interactive television to offer a physics class to three other high schools. Two more courses were developed for 1989–1990.

Burris is also reevaluating its role in applied research and curriculum development. Providing clinical experiences has always been the school's main function, but a stronger thrust in research and development is being encouraged to increase Burris's potential for service to education.

Laboratory schools seem to be forever in transition; Burris is no exception. Support from the university and college administration is strong. Burris continues to be blessed with outstanding faculty who are not only scholars in their fields but also excellent teachers and teacher educators. Parents' support for the school and its programs remains strong. Given this support and the school's record of accomplishment, there is reason to believe that many productive years are still ahead.

University School
Indiana State University
Terre Haute, Indiana

The University School is a primary site for pre–student-teaching experiences. Nearly two thirds of the university's observation and participation assignments take place in our classrooms. Activity is expanding in other areas of service, research, and publication.

The current program emphases include mainstreaming handicapped children into preschool learning environments, all-day kindergarten programs, whole-language instruction in elementary classes, foreign language instruction and research in grades K–6, oral communication, a gifted and talented program, and cross-age and peer-tutoring programs.

The school continues to support program development efforts of the state's education department. Faculty members serve as state consultants to local school districts, publishers of curriculum guides, contractors for in-service programs for teachers, and participants in accumulating baseline data for school improvement efforts.

The school is also nurturing contacts with sister schools in Jamaica, South America, the Philippines, and the People's Republic of China. The Jamaican instructional program is the model for our other activities, representing the benefits of joint programs at the elementary, secondary, and college levels.

The status of the school is enhanced by the relationship it enjoys with an expanding constituency. The administration of the university is seeking to improve the school's facilities, to define its role and mission in teacher education, and to expand its influence on public school systems through collaborative relationships and dissemination of programs and practices that benefit the school improvement effort.

IOWA

Malcolm Price Laboratory School
University of Northern Iowa
Cedar Falls, Iowa

This school is described in Chapter 3.

KANSAS

Butcher Children's School
Emporia State University
Emporia, Kansas

Every semester Butcher Children's School provides laboratory experiences for about eighty upper-division elementary education majors who spend ninety minutes a day for eight weeks observing and participating in classroom activity.

Observer-participants assigned to a specified grade work with a teacher who is an adjunct member of the university faculty. Observer-participants complete activities and acquire competences in

• awareness of child growth and development patterns as related to learning and behavior in the classroom.

- long-range planning and daily preparation for teaching content.
- techniques of classroom management.
- awareness of techniques for evaluating children's progress and a teacher's effectiveness.
- effective communication skills.
- professional behavior.

One required activity is teaching at least two lessons using the Madeline Hunter Lesson Planning Design. Observers attend biweekly group sessions with the supervisor of the observer-participant program at Butcher, where they address issues of curriculum approach, class management, discipline, and professionalism. Teachers supervise and evaluate the activities of observer-participants, helping them relate to students, locate and use materials, work with individuals and small groups, and learn management techniques.

KENTUCKY

Model Laboratory School
Eastern Kentucky University
Richmond, Kentucky

Model Laboratory School is the primary field site for all basic education courses in Eastern Kentucky University. Students complete observation and participation activities in cooperation with Model teachers. Their structured field experiences are keyed to basic concepts and skills according to a prescribed curriculum plan. Students use a handbook for each course to complete the activities as they proceed.

In addition, university students work with lab school teachers as part of other education courses to prepare them for teaching. In a single semester a thousand students may spend more than ten thousand hours in the school during the field components of their courses. Over the past decade the school's prime function has been to provide opportunities for pre-service teachers to learn and apply knowledge about teaching.

Model Laboratory School students in grade 10 have had the top achievement scores in the state for the past two years. Juniors and seniors consistently score well above the state and national averages on the SAT and ACT tests, with 100 percent participation in one or both testing programs. Exceptional students are totally mainstreamed, and the school offers a variety of enrichment and field experiences for all students.

The school has become a prominent resource for in-service programs for teachers in the region. Teachers from entire school districts come to the school for observation and in-service programs. Faculty members conduct on-site in-service programs in some subjects. The school works closely with the Kentucky education department as a trial and dissemination center. Its students are used in research studies by university faculty in education, psychology, and allied health.

LOUISIANA

University Laboratory School
Louisiana State University
Baton Rouge, Louisiana

The Louisiana State University Laboratory School opened in 1915 as the Demonstration High School. By 1923 it included grades 7 through 11. A full elementary program was added in 1936, grade 12 in 1945. During these expansions, the school's name was changed to University Laboratory School. The kindergarten program was added in 1981. Enrollment is 760 students.

The school has served as a site for student teaching, research, and a "model school" program. It now serves about two hundred undergraduate students a year in pre–student-teaching field experiences while accommodating over two thousand hours of classroom observations. University faculty and graduate students use the school's diverse population as research subjects. The school's faculty members develop innovative programs, which they disseminate, along with research findings, through in-service workshops and meetings of professional organizations.

The school's strengths are research and development in classroom management and study skills, sequential programs in reading for grades K–9, manipulative approaches to mathematics in grades K–5, development of an elementary science program emphasizing process skills, and well-rounded programs in music, English, science, athletics, and mathematics in the secondary school.

Honors in recent years include the Presidential Award for Excellence in Teaching Mathematics (1988 and 1989), the Presidential Award for Teaching Science (1983 and 1988), *Discover* magazine's Science Teacher of the Year award (1983), *Scholastic* magazine's Kids Care Winner (first grade, 1988–1989), and election of the first classroom teacher as president of the National Association of Colleges and Schools. Faculty members have also been selected for participation in Woodrow Wilson institutes (mathematics) and Rockefeller Fellowship programs (foreign language).

University Laboratory School
Southeastern Louisiana University
Hammond, Louisiana

The University Laboratory School at Southeastern Louisiana University serves as a research, development, and demonstration school, operating conjunctively with the university and the local public school system. The lab school wants children to grow up as broadly interested, deeply committed, healthy persons capable of interacting effectively with others. Therefore the primary work of this school is to supply an environment rich in resources for learning and to support the exploration of these resources so that students learn to cope successfully with the changing world in their own way and on their own terms.

The school recognizes that some common societal behavior patterns must be acknowledged if people are to live together in harmony. For this reason the environment gives students freedom in proportion to the degree of responsibility they show. The school aims to start students along the way to their lifelong pursuit of becoming. It provides beginnings from which students may move in different directions. In such an environment, designs for learning are relevant to children, helping them to succeed and prepare for the next steps.

Children entering grades 2 through 8 participate in the reading assessment and developmental reading program at the lab school during the summer. A series of tests assess their academic ability, reading interests, and reading effectiveness. The school furnishes to parents a written analysis of the results and sets an appointment to discuss the results.

During the three-week session, children learn to read by reading stories, writing, performing plays, telling stories, and doing other motivating activities. Workbook activities are not used. Parents get a written summary of the child's progress at the end of the program.

The summer kindergarten program is open to children who attended kindergarten the previous year or are eligible to attend kindergarten during the upcoming year. Two sessions are conducted, and children may attend one or both three-week sessions. Academic, social, and physical skills are also stressed to help children continue to progress through the summer and be well prepared in the fall.

A summer program lasting three weeks is open to gifted children entering grades 2 through 9. Eligibility is based on IQ scores, creativity, and/or characteristics consistent with success in the type of program offered. Participants do not have to be enrolled in a public school program for the gifted, but they must meet eligibility requirements.

A. E. Phillips Laboratory School
Louisiana Tech University
Ruston, Louisiana

From its beginning in 1916 the A. E. Phillips Laboratory School has been an integral part of the college of education at Louisiana Tech University. The school enrolls students from kindergarten through grade 8. Programs in art, music, and physical education, taught by certified instructors, are available at all grade levels. Enrichment offerings in the middle grades include fine arts, foreign language, and computer literacy.

The school offers pre-service activities for college students, gives demonstration lessons, and develops innovative programs, which it disseminates, along with other research findings, through professional organizations and workshops. But the school also aims to provide a model educational experience for its students.

A. E. Phillips is uniquely situated and equipped to demonstrate the close correlation between theoretical concepts taught in college courses and practical application in schools. Among the factors that enhance the teacher preparation mission of the college are the school's commitment to its goals, state-of-the-art facilities, and proximity to the college.

MASSACHUSETTS

Burnell Campus School
Bridgewater State College
Bridgewater, Massachusetts

The Martha Burnell Laboratory School on the campus of Bridgewater State College was established by the college in the 1880s to advance teacher education. The school has a history of preparing outstanding teachers and designing advanced curricular programs and innovative instructional procedures.

It has also provided a superb education for public elementary school students. Its comprehensive facilities serve about four hundred students in day care through grade 6. Among its modern features are an art room, music room, gymnasium, solar greenhouse, and amphitheater. A sophisticated media center serves students, staff, and student teachers. The center has darkrooms, microcomputers, a television studio, and audiovisual equipment.

Teachers maintain model classrooms where they do demonstration teaching. Instructional models for maximum learning are developed by individual teachers and approved by the faculty. Teacher-made materials support instruction in all subject areas. The program of instruction uses the latest methodology and incorporates the newest materials published in subject areas.

The teaching staff consists of highly qualified people, most of whom have at least thirty hours of graduate study beyond a master's degree. Faculty members in their teacher-training role use education majors and student teachers in their classes—a beneficial arrangement for all. Pupils get more individual attention; teachers can attend to developing instructional programs; teacher preparation students profit from observing master teachers practicing their craft.

Elementary students are assigned to the school by the superintendent of Bridgewater schools. The academic education of its students is the top priority of this school. To ensure that students are challenged, they are assigned to small groups on the basis of specific needs in mathematics and reading. Three such groups are combined to form a class and assigned to a teacher as a base classroom. Students are assigned for indefinite periods and may be reassigned to another group or another classroom or grade according to progress and readiness. This flexibility allows the school to accommodate students' needs in each subject.

Because this system requires strong guidance, the school uses an innovative management system in reading and mathematics to plot each child's progress in these critical areas.

The Parent Advisory Council is an active participant in the Burnell Laboratory School. In addition, parents and retirees participate in unique projects: Computer Education, Junior Great Books, Library, Career Awareness, Media Club, Adopt-a-Grandparent, and the RSVP (Retired Senior Volunteer Program).

The physical education program at Burnell emphasizes skill development in three areas: games, dance, and gymnastics. Within each area, lessons focus on one or more aspects of movement:, (1) body awareness—what the body is doing; (2) spatial awareness—where the body is going; (3) effort awareness—how the body is moving; and (4) relationship awareness—what activity is being done with whom.

While teaching movement, the teacher works toward objectives in the psychomotor, cognitive, and affective domains. In the psychomotor domain, for example, the development of versatility, efficiency, and effectiveness in movement is paramount. Throughout the program, physical fitness is emphasized and developed. Health-related fitness testing in grades 5 and 6 further underscores the desirability of physical fitness.

A bright and spacious instructional resource center connects to most classrooms. In this center are the library, a TV studio, a materials preparation room, two darkrooms, and storage areas. Most reference books are on movable carts for easy access. Eleven custom-designed carrels are used for media viewing and listening, including closed-circuit television; four carrels are set up as a "prep center" for preparing materials. Two Apple computers are available in the library, one on a mobile cart. The darkrooms and TV studio are available for student and staff use. The resource center is an ideal spot for inter-action between future teachers and children.

Burnell Elementary School Television ("B.E.S.T.") is produced largely by an after-school production club of students in grades 3 to 6 who cover school and local events, review books and movies, and pro-duce segments on cooking, hobbies, science, health and safety, and more. Children get help from the school's media specialist, parents, and "alumni" volunteers in planning, writing, editing, camera work, sound and lighting, and preparing props and computer graphics.

MISSOURI

Horace Mann Learning Center
Northwest Missouri State University
Maryville, Missouri

The Horace Mann Learning Center on the campus of Northwest Missouri State University includes an early childhood program sponsored by the university's college of education and its college of agriculture and applied sciences. It furnishes clinical experience for students in both colleges, demonstrating seven preschool and day-care models. The program also seeks to contribute to improving child care by incorporating these features:

- To raise the status and professionalism of early childhood workers, we have prepared and used a job description for upgrading certification and licensing of early childhood educators and care providers.
- To strengthen the academic preparation of prospective early childhood professionals, we have designed and used a structured practicum with measurable outcomes. The training includes a mix of theory, research, and on-site experience. It requires participants to

review and report on current literature to stay in tune with the needs
of a changing society.

- Because parents and other persons who handle the primary care of
young children are their most influential and "natural" teachers,
they participate in the program to ensure optimal learning for each
child.

This program combines the early childhood program of the
school of education with the child care and parent education program
of the home economics department; hence it benefits from an array of
expertise and resources.

The Horace Mann Learning Center uses a comprehensive, developmentally based guidance program for the university lab school,
grades K through 6. The model, first and foremost a preventive program, depends on carefully identified objectives, performance indicators, evaluation outcomes, and accountability status reports. The value
of the model is that it identifies children's strengths rather than treat-
ing their "deficits."

The program links students, teachers, parents, and community
networks in a preventive effort to address learning delays and behav-
ioral delays. It is a practical model that can be adapted for use in elementary schools of all sizes. It meshes interpersonal and social guidance with a cognitive and affective curriculum that works in harmony
with other subject areas. It supports children with problems during
their formative years, and its monitoring system lets parents join in
taking responsibility for helping children meet goals.

Greenwood Laboratory School
Southwest Missouri State University
Springfield, Missouri

The Greenwood Laboratory School, operated by Southwest Missouri
State University, conducts research, develops curriculum, and
demonstrates educational practices. It serves pre-teaching students in
the college as a learning laboratory, college faculty members as a research laboratory, and its own students as the place to receive a comprehensive program of schooling.

The multiple missions of Greenwood depend on close communication and interaction among all the the school's constituents.
The school's seventy-eight-year tradition of excellence and opportunity for advancement in education is the cornerstone that connects the
college educational community with the community it serves.

The school features some innovations for its own staff and students and for staff and students of other schools in Missouri.

Because one mission of the school is to review curriculum
goals and find innovative ways to meet them, several elementary instructors undertook a study of the reading curriculum. They have implemented a whole-language approach to reading and writing in which
children are not grouped by ability and use almost no workbooks or
skill sheets.

Students at Greenwood use teleconferencing to interview con-
gressmen, officials, authors, scientists, TV news correspondents, and
other celebrities. These interviews are conducted via a speakerphone in
the classroom.

During the past four years, Greenwood has been developing an
administrative software package to meet the needs of small schools.
Records are maintained for all students. The program stores students'
names, identification numbers, addresses, parents' names, alternative
addresses, county of residence, and emergency contacts. From this
information the program can produce grade-level lists and mailing
lists that can be alphabetized, printed by class, or printed by school
level.

The school sponsors a marine biology course at Hofstra
University's marine biological station at St. Ann Bay in Jamaica. The
resident marine biologist at the station alters a college curriculum to
meet the needs of our students in grades 9 through 12. The primary objective of the program is to expose "landlocked" students to shore,
ocean, lagoon, and reef environments. The lessons center on field
trips, snorkeling, laboratory work, and discussions. A bonus is that students become aware of cultural differences between Jamaica and the
United States.

The school and the university together sponsor an annual ski trip to Steamboat Springs, Colorado, for grades 9 through 12. Students get not only experience in skiing but also the opportunity to live for a week with peers in a condominium at the resort.

For public school juniors and seniors, Greenwood offers a two-week social studies class on Japan, including a seventeen-day tour. Ten days of classes introduce the geography, history, government, economics, and culture of Japan, along with daily instruction in Japanese.

The Southwest Missouri Young Authors Conference each year honors about 750 young authors from the area who have written, edited, illustrated, and "published" compositions. On a Saturday in the spring, these writers, from elementary grades 1 to 6, come to the university campus to represent their fellow writers in eighty schools in the twenty-four-county area. Greenwood Laboratory School, the university's departments of reading and special education, and the Springfield chapter of the International Reading Association have sponsored the conference since its inception in 1981. Some 180 area teachers serve as coordinators and small-group leaders, and about 180 SMSU students serve as assistants.

The College School
Webster College
Webster Groves, Missouri

The College School of Webster Groves exemplifies achievement and productivity through experiential education. After eight thousand unsuccessful tries on a nickel-iron storage battery, Thomas Edison was heard to say, "Well, at least we know eight thousand things that won't work." After twenty-one years of experiencing and risk-taking, we at The College School know at least eight thousand things that do work. Because we believe that educators need to be problem solvers and entrepreneurs, we support and champion innovative teaching and learning.

Working from the laboratory model, we have established our identity and our mission. The laboratory model is best explained by our operating practices:

- Championing new ideas. We support experimentation by teachers and administrators. Failure is not a negative.
- Cooperative teaming. We support a team approach to teaching, learning, and problem solving. Our practice involves the entire school, from principal through teachers, parents, and students.
- Being pro-active and experiential. We support learning and teaching that is oriented to action and participation.

The response of our school has always differed from the traditional. In a vastly changing society, schools must be responsive. Marshall McLuhan said, "You can't drive into the future looking out the rearview mirror." The College School offers a positive attitude about the future, about change, and about learning and teaching. We try always to look directly through our windshield.

As a laboratory school, The College School provides and strengthens understanding of how children learn and how to teach most effectively. Our major strengths lie in developing instructional materials, in case studies, in research, and in application. These strengths enable us to excel in staff development, customized and responsive in-service training, and production of curriculum materials and products.

NEW HAMPSHIRE

Wheelock School
Keene State College
Keene, New Hampshire

Wheelock School is the laboratory school for Keene State College. It became a training school when Keene opened as a normal school in 1909. The normal school was located in Keene because of the willingness of the local community and school system to form a cooperative arrangement. The college and the district have both benefited for more than seventy years from this relationship. Children in the school live in the area surrounding the school, thus providing a cross section of Keene's population. Children from other areas of the city may attend if space is available.

Under the agreement between the school district and the college, responsibilities are shared as follows:

- The district provides the facilities, maintenance, special services such as health and lunch programs, and transportation for pupils.
- The college maintains an approved elementary school for grades K through 5 plus classes for special needs, staffs it with competent and qualified teachers, and equips it with up-to-date educational materials and equipment.
- The school system and the college are jointly responsible for supervision of the school, curriculum, classification and promotion of pupils, and general regulations.
- The supervisory union pays the college at the end of each quarter for the education of pupils assigned to the Wheelock School. The figure is based on the salaries the Wheelock staff would earn if employed by the district minus 10 percent plus a sum for educational supplies and equipment.
- The college adds 10 to 15 percent over the annual cost of operation to provide additional equipment and to foster innovation and research.

In Wheelock's "Write On with Us" program, faculty and principal make two-year commitments to the writing process. Monthly workshops built around the theme "What Works for You?" provide continuing analysis and a supportive environment. The process provides opportunities for writing, reading, editing, spelling awareness, oral expression, active listening, and developing research skills. Self-evaluation, peer evaluation, group conferencing, and teacher feedback create acceptance and support while building the young writer's self-concept. Some children write or edit their pieces on a computer. When a child publishes, a second copy goes to the school library for circulation among the children.

Because all Wheelock teachers are deeply involved in the writing process, "whole language" instruction in reading seems a natural extension.

Audiovisual recordings are being used to enhance instructional skills, help teachers evaluate themselves, and maintain public relations. This program earned a Center of Excellence award from the National Council of Teachers of English.

The drug program at Wheelock gives pupils information about the effects of drugs and explores why people take them. The curriculum emphasizes self-concept, social skills, and coping skills. It teaches that alcohol and drug dependence are treatable diseases.

NEW YORK

College Learning Laboratory
Buffalo State College
Buffalo, New York

This school is described in the latter part of Chapter 3.

Hunter College Campus Schools
Hunter College
New York, New York

Hunter College Campus Schools, elementary and secondary, are among the oldest self-contained schools for intellectually gifted students in the nation. The schools, chartered by the trustees of the City University of New York and administered by Hunter College, are publicly funded.

Admission to the schools is by examination and demonstrated academic promise. The racial and ethnic makeup of New York City is maintained. About 40 percent of the students come from minority groups. The schools use an outreach program to attract economically disadvantaged minority students who are gifted.

The high school offers a rigorous, traditional college-preparatory course of study. The school's philosophy holds that bright, inquisitive minds must be thoroughly informed and trained. Classes are marked by lively interchanges among students and between students and teachers. Learning to communicate effectively permeates the curriculum. An extensive extracurricular program insures that students have the opportunity for a well-rounded education.

Inter–College Year (ICY) provides a unique opportunity for students to continue their intellectual and personal development through a project. Students enroll in a minimum of two courses, one of which must be for advanced placement or college credit; as part of their coursework, students plan individual projects.

In conjunction with Hunter College, the elementary school strives to be a model of excellence in educating gifted youngsters by providing them with educational experiences appropriate to their individual abilities, interests, and learning styles. Because the school respects and welcomes individual uniqueness, it stresses creative effort, intellectual initiative, independent study, critical thinking, social adjustment, social responsibility, and leadership development.

The environment in the elementary school is conducive to studying and learning, with ample activities for enrichment. The curriculum is constantly being revised to accommodate change and growth. Because gifted students are quick learners, the school takes an open, flexible approach to new ideas.

The elementary science program aims to cultivate the attitudes, skills, and concepts necessary to understand the workings of our world. The program is concerned more with seeing, thinking, and doing than with mastering facts.

Central to the program is the belief that attitudes are acquired rather than learned. Among the attitudes sought are curiosity, originality, cooperation, perseverance, open-mindedness, self-criticism, and independence in thinking. Skills are embedded in the framework of the scientific method. Through a variety of learning situations, students develop skill in observing, hypothesizing, estimating, testing, measuring, communicating, recording, comparing, classifying, and concluding. Concepts that are developed at each grade level are in harmony with the science being studied.

NORTH DAKOTA

University Laboratory School
Minot State University
Minot, North Dakota

The University Laboratory School, for children from pre-kindergarten through grade 6, is organized for maximum flexibility to adapt to experimental projects. Seven teachers are responsible for 189 students. Classes typically contain fifty children in two grades, with two teachers sharing instructional duties. Children are admitted by date of application and pay a modest tuition. Each professional staff member holds at least a master's degree and accepts the tripartite mission of teaching, service, and research.

The quality of teaching is worthy of study and emulation by the profession. Of students who transfer to public junior high schools, 70 percent make the honor roll their first year.

Service to the profession takes several forms. Staff members present their research findings at local, state, and national professional meetings; they offer in-service instruction to staffs of local school districts in North Dakota and in Canada; they assume leadership in assisting underserviced populations in the state through the Gifted Education Network maintained by the staff at the lab school. The school is also the dominant force in gifted education in the state.

Research and innovation are the overarching purposes of the school. Its goal is to provide better education to the children of the state by bringing promising ideas into operational practice. The staff at this school showed the value and effectiveness of integrating a kindergarten for four-year-old children in 1968; it demonstrated the practicality of mainstreaming educable mentally handicapped children into regular classrooms in 1970.

Now the teachers are redefining ways that generate learning in elementary classes by multi-age grouping of children with two teacher teams, individualizing instruction for every child, integrating gifted education into the regular classroom, developing a continuum for computer literacy starting at age four, identifying individual learning styles and capitalizing on them to maximize learning, replacing textbook instruction by using library materials and other primary and secondary sources, and reporting children's progress by a narrative report form.

A host of projects and studies are planned, including descriptive studies of teaching reading (and other subjects) without a textbook, analytic studies of multi-age groups, individualized instruction, and a host of other topics.

Postscript: The laboratory school at Minot was closed by the university at the end of the 1989–1990 school year because of a shortage of funds.

PENNSYLVANIA

Miller Research Learning Center
Edinboro University of Pennsylvania
Edinboro, Pennsylvania

The Miller Research Learning Center is an early childhood learning center with a focus on whole-language instruction. The center comprises a day care center, with 150 children from fourteen months to five years, and the Miller School, with sixty children from preschool through grade 4.

Miller is shifting its focus to whole-language development and instruction. It aims to serve more students of elementary education methods in clinical class experiences and to serve as a center for demonstrating staff development and appraisal for northwest Pennsylvania.

New funding for the Pennsylvania Consortium of Laboratory Schools will enable the state's laboratory schools to collaborate on research and development and to work with institutions that do not have laboratory schools.

University School
Indiana University of Pennsylvania
Indiana, Pennsylvania

The University School at Indiana University of Pennsylvania is a department within the college of education. It has operated continuously for 113 years. Children attend from six school districts. Nearly 60 percent of the students come from families that have no affiliation with the university.

Unlike many laboratory schools, this school is not just a student-teaching site. Instead, it is a laboratory of human resources for faculty and students in the college, for its own teachers and students, and for teachers, parents, and administrators in basic education in western Pennsylvania. Faculty members and students from other colleges in the university visit to observe, participate, and engage in research with children. Four doctoral students relieve four faculty members, enabling them to do educational research.

Teachers in the school hold faculty status in the university. Some teach in other departments. Many members of other colleges and departments in the university hold dual status in the school.

In a single school year the University School recorded 15,648 visitors. Most of the visits included interactions with children.

The school has created, revised, and modeled many innovative programs in Pennsylvania. In cooperation with the college and the state, the school is modeling two programs for special students—a mixed category (mainstreamed) program and a program for hearing-impaired students. Beyond this, an innovative K–6 curriculum has been developed and published in *Computer Instruction*. Faculty members are writing a full description of the reading and language arts programs that will highlight innovations at each level. And the music department has designed an instrumental music program that uses a multisensory approach to make music accessible to students with hearing or learning disabilities.

The school networks by computer with U.S. laboratory schools; it links with Shanghai Teachers University in foreign language and culture programs. Texts in Chinese language and culture have been developed by Jiang Zhi, a visiting scholar from this university. *A Guide to Thematic Teaching about China in American Schools* was written by John Johnson, Wenju Shen, and Donald McFeely.

The school accommodates a large load of observation and participation assignments. All elementary majors during their first two years are required to work with children in the school. During the senior year a few student teachers (one per faculty member) are assigned to the school, some as members of a team that includes a master teacher (a full-time faculty member), a teaching associate (a doctoral student), and a student teacher.

Children's School
Carnegie Mellon University
Pittsburgh, Pennsylvania

This school is described in the latter part of Chapter 3.

Falk School
University of Pittsburgh
Pittsburgh, Pennsylvania

Falk School performs the customary functions of laboratory schools: research to improve instruction and learning, demonstration of effective teaching practices, services to university students, and schooling from kindergarten through grade 8.

The school accommodates differences in students' needs, interests, abilities, talents, and styles of learning by a scheme that features multi-age grouping, nongraded classes, and team teaching. Instruction stresses inquiry and critical thinking. As the school works to refine its program to meet the needs of many constituencies, its faculty and school board review instructional models that are consistent with the school's philosophy and have sufficient merit to warrant investigation.

Falk School also houses an internship for college graduates with degrees in liberal arts or a professional field. The program, for a master of arts in teaching, is built on extended practical experience in the laboratory school. It focuses on skills essential for effective teaching, incorporating mechanisms designed to ensure that introspection, research, and planned change are integral to the program. The design includes study of the program's impact on the lab school, behavior changes among the program's participants, and ongoing examination of the model.

Expectation of change is implicit in our laboratory school. The curriculum, the organization, and the instructional design are subject to continuing revision and, if called for, even radical change.

Rowland School for Young Children
Shippensburg University
Shippensburg, Pennsylvania

Rowland School, on the campus of Shippensburg University, operates through a cooperative agreement between the university and the school district. The school enrolls children from kindergarten through grade 6. The university also supports a tuition-based nursery program for two sections of four-year-old children.

The cooperative agreement specifies that the school's director, administrative assistant, and teachers of kindergarten and grades 1 and 2 are to be employed by the university as tenured members of the teacher education department. Teachers of grades 3 to 6 are to be employed by the school district. Each group of faculty is governed by its own contract guidelines. The district provides instruction in art, music, and physical education; the university covers costs of interns, graduate counseling, library instruction, and teaching of swimming and foreign languages by university students.

Rowland presents opportunities for students majoring in teaching, psychology, and sociology to observe and participate in supervised activities with children. It also develops, tests, and disseminates new curricula. Its faculty members also field-test new curricula developed elsewhere and collaborate with university faculty members on grant-supported curriculum projects. In addition, teachers plan total units of special study for each academic year.

The school population is based on parent interest. Rowland is a public school for students who live in the school district; the district charges tuition for students residing outside the district.

An advisory council of parents, teachers, school district representatives, and faculty members in teacher education advises the school on policy development. Parents provide a strong base of support for the school, participating regularly as aides in classes and helping with regularly scheduled school activities such as field trips, outdoor education, and special units.

School for Exceptional Children
Slippery Rock State University
Slippery Rock, Pennsylvania

The School for Exceptional Children began in 1965 as a joint venture of Slippery Rock University and the Grove City Association for the Mentally Retarded and Physically Handicapped. In June 1966 the university was licensed by the Pennsylvania department of education to operate a private academic school serving exceptional children. The school was granted public school status in 1968. From the beginning, the university attempted to develop a mutually beneficial relationship with the public school systems in the region. Over the years the joint venture has served students from seven districts.

The school is an essential part of the university's program for preparing special-education teachers, and it figures in the districts' long-range planning for the education of exceptional children.

The university provides three full-time faculty positions to the school, and members of the special-education department serve the school as consultants on its program. The university furnishes three classrooms, offices, and other space plus secretarial and custodial services.

The districts provide transportation for their pupils and coordinate placement and psychological services. They cover the costs of instructional materials and supplies and the salary of the teacher aide.

The primary program is carefully structured to meet desirable and realistic goals based on knowledge of the developmental progression in motor skills, social interests and experiences, and receptive and expressive functioning. Planning learning activities for children depends on knowing, for each one, what their motor capacity is, knowing how to capture their attention and interest, and knowing what they can understand and express. The program focuses on self-help skills, survival words, language, self-image, body awareness and environmental awareness, gross and fine motor skills, writing skills, aesthetics, and spatial, auditory, and visual discrimination. Children move ahead at their own rate.

In the secondary program, students spend half the day in an academic program and half in a prevocational workshop. According to their needs, they get individual or small-group instruction in auditory perception, visual perception, communication, language, writing, typing, vocabulary, math, concepts, reading, and computer programs. Music and art classes are presented at holiday times. In the prevocational workshop more than thirty work stations provide experience and training in such skills as sorting, assembly, packaging, and production. Teacher trainees monitor their progress on such work behaviors as punctuality, responsibility, taking supervision, following directions, and cooperating with co-workers and supervisors.

The school also provides practicum experiences for university students. Over a hundred undergraduates each semester volunteer as aides. Depending on their majors, they assist with physical education and adaptive swimming, music therapy, physical therapy, and health screening. Some sixty teacher trainees in special education handle one-on-one and small-group instruction in classrooms and workshops.

SOUTH CAROLINA

Felton Laboratory School
South Carolina State College
Orangeburg, South Carolina

Innovative, flexible, and creative describe the administration, faculty, and student body of Felton Laboratory School. The school's $700,000 complex was built in 1964 on the beautiful, landscaped campus of South Carolina State College. Originally called the Felton Training

School, this lab school grew from a kindergarten program developed in 1920. The school grew along with the department of education in the college as courses in methods, observation, and directed teaching were added. A four-room building was donated for teacher education in 1924. Today Felton Laboratory School accommodates youngsters from kindergarten through eighth grade. They are selected by application. The school participates in the state's testing program.

The school continues to serve the teacher education program at the college, serving as a professional laboratory where teacher education majors gain expertise through clinical experiences. The school also serves as a center for research in child growth and development.

The lower school follows a continuous-progress model in which teaching and administrative procedures are adjusted to accommodate differences among students. The middle school continues the pattern, with individualization, team teaching, pupil pairing, and flexible grouping. Felton attends to the unique needs of middle school children by offering several exploratory and special-interest courses. The exploratory courses are art, music, physical education, foreign language, and career development. Among the special-interest courses are band, art appreciation, mixed chorus, sewing, drama, and broadcasting.

Felton students, known as the "Junior Bulldogs," are part of all programs held on the South Carolina State campus. They attend lyceum programs and athletic contests; they visit the planetarium, art museum, and theater. The broadcasting class presents a weekly program on WSSB, the college radio station.

The Felton family is proud of two additional programs in the school: "Kids In Kollege" and "The Afternoon School." The first is a six-week summer workshop in basic skills for students entering grades 2 to 9. It is open to students who attend any school in the area. In The Afternoon School, which operates from 2:45 to 5:00 Monday through Thursday, students get instruction in basic school subjects.

On the professional staff are the director and assistant director, a media specialist, a guidance coordinator, and twenty-eight full-time teachers.

TENNESSEE

University School
Eastern Tennessee State University
Johnson City, Tennessee

The University School at Eastern Tennessee State University offers a K–12 program.

A special feature of this school is a once-a-month program of activities offered by resource people in the university and the community for grades 1 to 6. Students have a choice of programs. A large resource file has been assembled for this purpose. This program has served as a model for other schools, and the resource file has been made available to them.

The University School environment promotes success in academic competition. Its Academic Decathlon Teams were state champions in 1986 and 1987. They came in sixteenth nationally in 1986, tenth in 1987. The school had the Citizen Bee Social Studies state champion in 1987 and the Veterans of Foreign Wars state essay winner in 1988. Its speech and drama teams have always been strong, with one or more state winners a year.

Homer Pittard Campus School
Middle Tennessee State University
Murfreesboro, Tennessee

Homer Pittard Campus School exists for a twofold purpose: to serve children in the Rutherford County school system who enroll in grades K–6 and to serve as an instructional laboratory for teacher education.

The school promotes students' development in all growth areas—physical, intellectual, social, and emotional. The faculty believes that the curriculum should enable children to develop and maintain positive feelings toward themselves. Finally, the faculty believes that all children should be guided to achieve to the best of their ability. Because there is no single way to carry out these goals, teachers constantly employ multiple instructional alternatives.

Homer Pittard Campus School is embedded in the university's department of elementary and special education. The Campus School is a built-in laboratory where prospective teachers can interact with children every day, getting ample opportunity to learn teaching skills and develop competence under master teachers. Campus School faculty members are clinical instructors for the university's department of education. Each faculty member teaches at least one elementary methods course at the school each academic year.

University students in the kindergarten practicum work with students and teachers in classrooms throughout the semester. Methods students hear lectures on teaching approaches for each subject, observe demonstration lessons taught by faculty members in specified grades, and then teach a lesson using the method studied and observed.

The needs of the university's teacher education program determine the enrollment ceiling and distribution. Each grade has two classes of twenty-five to thirty students. The school has a minority-group enrollment nearly proportional to the county's population. As long as Campus School is designated a "cluster school" for the county's intellectually gifted students, second priority will be given to 10 percent of the enrollment for students certified in this category.

All grade levels adhere to state and county basic skills sequences in all instructional areas. The physical education curriculum meets local, state, and national guidelines but offers more variety to meet the needs of the children and the roles of the university and county system in providing exemplary programs. For games and sports, students in grades 1 to 6 can choose cooperative or competitive learning tracks. Gymnastics and dance are standard parts of the program for all children.

University students in music education participate in and teach music classes, getting hands-on experience with children. All children in grades K–6 get instruction in general music, singing, playing instruments, moving to music, creating their own music, and hearing and analyzing styles of music. Children in grades 4–6 have extra training weekly in school choral ensembles. An after-school choir and instrumental ensemble is open to youngsters in grades 5 and 6. The choirs have performed across the eastern United States for choral festivals and music conventions. Campus School children may be heard on the records accompanying the Silver Burdett and Ginn *World of Music* textbook series.

The school's art program, directed by a full-time university professor, fosters creative abilities along with a lasting appreciation of art.

The school offers a good many special programs. Among them are Fabulous Fridays, an annual spring event in which students select the courses to be taught; a Junior Great Books program; special projects on schoolwide interests, such as Nutrition and Earth Day; and an Odyssey of the Mind program led by parents.

A resource teacher at the school helps teachers with exceptional children who need specially tailored learning experiences. The library/media specialist assists in enrichment activities and coordinates schoolwide contests and literary competitions, such as the annual Raintree publish-a-book contest, the local Reading Association book-writing contests, and the Volunteer State student book selection.

A National Geographic Bee was held this year for grades 4 to 6. Campus School participates annually in the county's spelling bee and the university-sponsored math contest for sixth-graders. Sixth-graders also compete in the Science Bowl in May, and the school held its first annual Science Extravaganza this year.

Special features of Campus School include the Bradley Computer Laboratory, where children learn to use this new basic tool. Future teachers are required to complete a unit of work using computers in instruction. In 1989 the state's board of education designated Campus School as a Basic Skills First Exemplary School.

Campus School has always been blessed with an interested, enthusiastic parent group. Parents have covered costs of instructional materials and equipment and built a playground and amphitheater. They donate their time and expertise through well-coordinated and innovative events and assist with tutoring, field trips, and classroom projects.

UTAH

Edith Bowen Laboratory School
Utah State University
Logan, Utah

The Edith Bowen Laboratory School (K–5) is an integral part of Utah State University's award-winning elementary teacher education program. Before they do their student teaching, about 160 college juniors receive an academic quarter of experience in classrooms, where intensive instruction in methods fuses with experience in practicums.

The lab school was founded in 1928 as the Whittier Training School. Thirty years later the Edith Bowen Laboratory School was built on the university campus. Since then it has served as a center for undergraduate observation, early practicum experiences, graduate research, college and elementary instruction, and demonstration, development, and dissemination.

Edith Bowen students are selected from three school districts through an open application system. They represent a variety of intellectual, socioeconomic, and cultural backgrounds. A 15 percent foreign student population is enrolled at the school. The school is expanding from 270 to 350 students, and its building is being remodeled while a new building for the college goes up next to it.

As the sole lab school in Utah, Edith Bowen carries responsibility for developing and implementing innovative programs that can be adapted for use in regular schools. The school has designed model programs in individualized instruction, gifted and talented education, education through the arts, and computer-technological literacy.

The school is embarking on a new project in science, technology, and society for elementary schools. It is doing work on experiential learning processes, thinking skills programming, and clinical knowledge and skills for pre-service teachers.

The school's director has department head status within the college of education and reports directly to its dean. Basic support for the school comes from the university, the state's office of education, and flow-through monies from the districts. Additional funds come from private and grant sources.

An advisory board representing the state, the university, public schools, and the community assists the school in making decisions about program and operations. The board has set four basic goals for the school:

- to provide a high-quality educational program for the elementary school students enrolled at the school
- to provide a quality instructional and clinical laboratory setting for both undergraduate and graduate university students enrolled in professional preparation programs in elementary education and re-lated fields
- to provide a laboratory setting where research in educational pro-grams, issues, and trends related to elementary education and re-lated fields can be conducted
- to disseminate broadly throughout the state and nation the results of research-and-development activities

WASHINGTON

Robert Reid Laboratory School
Eastern Washington University
Cheney, Washington

Eastern Washington University's Robert Reid Lab School is best known for its high-quality instructional program for children. The school has served the university's teacher education program since 1892 as its site for laboratory experiences, curriculum development, and project dissemination.

In 1986 Reid School became a part of the Cheney public school district. Administration, staffing, admission of pupils, and cur-riculum planning are under the auspices of the local superintendent and board. The school's excellent observation tower facility responds to university needs with ease, and the university enjoys its young part-nership with local school people and programs.

A strong feature of the school is its ability to assist university students in learning to teach reading. Some 80 percent of the candidates for elementary teaching certificates at the university major in reading. The lab school offers the prerequisite reading practicum experiences.

In 1985 Reid was chosen by the National Council of Teachers of English as a National Center of Excellence in Language Arts for its unique approach in integrating the language arts.

Reid School is emerging as a research site. Several applied-research projects are completed each year. Reid staff members collaborate with professors from education, math, health, applied psychology, speech pathology, home economics, and other departments to generate relevant applied research. Their research efforts are targeted at building a bridge from experimental research to classroom application.

WYOMING

University School
University of Wyoming
Laramie, Wyoming

University School has existed at the University of Wyoming in one form or another since the university's inception over a hundred years ago. When the university was just a solitary building on the prairie, its first students did not all hold high school diplomas, so a "preparatory course" was begun to bring those with eighth-grade educations up to speed for college coursework. The name "Prep" has stuck in informal usage.

After the turn of the century, when the university began to train teachers, it needed a model school or practice site for practicum experiences. Thus Prep became a laboratory school similar to the one Dewey designed at Chicago. The first director of Prep in its incarnation as a lab school in the 1930s was a woman who taught children and directed teacher education activities at the university. This became the pattern at the school in the decades when Prep was moved to different facilities as the campus grew. The school and its personnel changed with the times by experimenting and promoting educational innovations, among them open classrooms, individually guided education, and middle school approaches.

Today the school is housed on two floors of the Education Building in the heart of the teacher education facilities, which occupy three buildings on the campus. Children, young people, university students, and faculty mingle daily because they all use the resources of the building.

Prep faculty are members of the department of curriculum and instruction, with a number of Ph.D.s in the ranks. As a laboratory site, the school has four major functions:

- to serve as a center for educating children and youth in experimental and innovative ways by maintaining a center for educational inquiry, developing prototypes or models of educational practices, and implementing experimental pre-service programs for teachers
- to serve as a clinical laboratory for teachers in preparation by providing classroom participation experiences, opportunities to use technology in teacher preparation, and resources for college classes in teacher education
- to serve as a laboratory for experimental research and evaluation by designing and implementing pilot activities for schools and teacher education programs and by designing and implementing evaluation systems for experimental programs
- to disseminate laboratory school programs and practices by serving as consultants, conducting workshops and in-service programs, opening the school to observation and discussion of innovative practices, and developing publications for dissemination to the profession

Prep has about twenty regular faculty and an enrollment of about 260 students from nursery through grade 9; plans are in progress to reinstate the secondary program. Teaching teams work with "units"—multi-age groups of children. Unit I corresponds loosely to grades 1 to 3, Unit 2 to grades 4 and 5, and Unit III to grades 6 to 9. For most learning activities, students are mixed in heterogeneous and cross-age groups.

Special features of the school program include an open-ended curriculum (no grade-level designations), individualized instruction (for intern projects and experimental practica), a "centers" approach to instruction (joint planning of activities around a common theme), and cooperative instructional activities (to promote responsibility for one's own learning).

Among other unique features in the school's program are foreign language offerings for preschool through grade 9, a whole-language approach to instruction, keyboarding for children beginning at age four, a model middle school program, instrumental and vocal music open to everyone, an art program integrated into other curricular areas, downhill skiing and swimming as part of the physical education program, town meetings about possible changes in the school or its program, and participation in activities such as National History Day, Young Authors, and science fairs.

Prep's students are selected by several criteria. For teacher education programs, it needs students of all ability levels to reflect the larger community. Students from multicultural or international backgrounds may take priority to counterbalance Laramie's mostly white population. The school aims for a stable long-term population, needed for its research and teacher education programs. The school tries to limit the proportion of students from university-related families—a difficult task because the university is Laramie's main employer.

The school is carrying on its tradition of experimentation and innovation through its participation in the National Network for Educational Renewal, a federal project spearheaded by Dr. John Goodlad. The Wyoming Partnership in the National Network has established ties among eight public school districts and the university. Improving teacher education programs and restructuring public schools are the major thrusts of the project, and Prep, as a demonstration partnership school, is at the center of such activities.

7

Campus Schools in the United States to 1965

Excerpts from
"Historical Background of the Campus School in America"

Harry Hutton

Schools established as handmaidens to teacher-training schools have gone by many names: model school, practice school, experimental school, laboratory school, and campus school. At first they were linked to normal schools—those barely respectable institutions pioneered in the United States between 1840 and 1880 when the idea gained currency that teachers should be trained.

Harry Hutton, late of Pennsylvania State University, traced the interlocking histories—and pedagogical styles—of training schools and their adjunct schools in a chapter he wrote for a 1965 book. From that chapter we have excerpted these pieces about the origins and the checkered progress of schools affiliated with normal schools and their more respectable descendants—state teachers colleges and colleges of education in universities.

OUR FIRST TEACHER-TRAINING INSTITUTIONS were destined to labor under many handicaps. . . . Resented by academies and scorned by colleges, having to make their way for years before any state legislature dreamed of setting any requirements for certification, the normals were essentially dead-end schools (Boyden 1933). They were post-elementary, semi-secondary at best, but in no way connected with higher education. . . . So slowly did the whole teacher-training movement gain ground in Massachusetts that it was not until 1904 that 50 percent of the teachers in the Commonwealth (7,392 out of 14,741) had attended normal school, of whom 42.7 percent had actually graduated (Mangun 1928). . . .

THE MODEL SCHOOL'S ORIGINAL FUNCTIONS

A standard feature of the pioneer normal [school] . . . was the model school or department. In its simplest form it was a roomful of elementary pupils more or less like those to be found in a district school. On a more ambitious scale it consisted of several rooms on a graded system.

The "model" idea was exemplified in three ways. There was model teaching, often by the normal school principal himself. There was model discipline. And there was model equipment. If the latter originally signified nothing much beyond a real blackboard, serviceable seats, a globe and a couple of maps, it represented a sound and promising principle. Somewhere along the line it was either forgotten or taken as a goal achieved. Had teacher-training institutions considered it a prime duty across the years to keep abreast of "model equipment," they would not be open to the charge of failing to exploit the possibilities of the phonograph, the motion picture, the radio, and other special media.

Priority was soon given to demonstrating perfect teaching and control. Since it is axiomatic that perfection cannot be improved, the master had no need to experiment. He gave demonstrations of an ideal "method," conceivably of different methods (e.g., lecture or recitation), and was closely observed by the normal school students, who eventually tried their hands at practice teaching and were judged against the standard set by the expert. In some institutions there was a practice school as well as a demonstration school. But *mutatis mutandis,* a master teacher, later to assume the role of critic, demonstrated ideal teaching and classroom control before an audience likely to be exhaustively divisible into mere boys and girls recently graduated from elementary school and some older students who had taught for a while and then decided, out of ambition or desperation, to see if a short sojourn at a normal school would be of any use to them. Since attendance was voluntary, one student might stay for a year, another for a few weeks.

It was a long time before the normals were firmly enough established and of sufficient prestige to have entrance requirements of any significance or to extend the course to two years, let alone three or four. Albany set a rigorous standard in 1890 by demanding high school graduation and made a verbal breakthrough by substituting "experimental" for "model" school. . . .

The late 1880s and the 1890s in American teacher education were years when the profession undoubtedly gained sorely needed prestige and when the subject of education itself was widely deemed to be worthy of a place on university timetables. It would be gratifying to add that . . . normal schools and their model schools gave vigorous leadership in developing a science of education whose hallmarks were research and experimentation. . . . [But] no rash of experimentation broke out. High school enrollment started its sky-rocketing rise in the 1890s and there was an inevitable improvement in the academic qualifications of the young men and women entering normal schools.

[Charles] De Garmo had passed a sharp judgment in the late 1880s. "Whatever the average American normal school may now be," he said, "in its very recent past it might have been fitly defined as a high school with a training attachment, having the limitations of a low-grade high school, and the ambitions of a high-grade college" (National Education Association 1887, 489). Nicholas Murray Butler was less severe. He was bound to admit, however, that he thought of normal schools as "academies or high schools with a slight infusion of pedagogic instruction" (Pangburn 1932, 29).

There was undoubted improvement in the 1890s. . . . Iowa, Michigan and Wisconsin were among the first of the better-known universities to enter the field, the former two in the 1870s. . . . [But] there is

no recorded story of cooperation or of good communication between
normal schools and institutions of higher education engaged in the
training of teachers. Nor was there any noticeable competition in anything that might pass for experimentation or the testing of fresh
ideas. . . .

THE NEW PEDAGOGY AND THE NEW LABORATORY SCHOOL

When John Dewey launched his famous laboratory school at the
University of Chicago in 1896, he broke sharply with the normal
school-model school tradition. He apparently found little in it that he
was eager to retain. . . . Mayhew and Edwards (1936/1965) have given us
the complete story of the famous laboratory school. Their book may
be taken as authoritative; it bears, indeed, the *imprimatur* of John
Dewey. Three of Mayhew and Edwards' statements are of particular
importance. And it may be observed, parenthetically, that part of the
first and all of the third are in line with the view that many educators
have today [that is, in the mid-1960s] of a campus school that they can
support.

1. "The school was a laboratory for the Department of
   Psychology and Pedagogy where Mr. Dewey's educational
   theories and their sociological implications were worked
   out in accord with the then-new psychological principles
   and in association with colleagues and students, the teachers in the school, and the parents of the pupils. It was
   never a 'practice school.' " (1936, v)

2. "The main hypothesis was that life itself, especially those
   occupations and associations which serve man's chief
   needs, should furnish the ground experience for the education of children." (1936, vi)

3. "Conducted under the management and supervision of the
   university's Department of Philosophy, Psychology, and
   Education, it bore the same relation to the work of the department that a laboratory bears to biology, physics, or
   chemistry. Like any such laboratory, it had two main purposes: (*a*) to exhibit, test, verify and criticize theoretical

statements and principles and (*b*) to add to the sum of
facts and principles in its special line." (1936, 3)

The activities of Dewey's school were of an amazing number
and variety. A modern teacher will note with relief that in 1902, when
the pupils reached their maximum total of one hundred and forty, "the
teaching staff increased to twenty-three teachers and instructors, with
about ten assistants (graduate students of the university)" (Mayhew and
Edwards 1936/1965, 8). But one can readily believe that all were busy
when he considers not only the classroom lessons and discussions, but
the field trips, the gardening, the cooking and weaving, the pottery, and
such a formidable undertaking as the furnishing and decorating of a
sizable clubhouse. The thirteen-year-olds experimented with simple
photography and every one of the eleven different "groups" had its
full quota of special experiences (Mayhew and Edwards 1936/1965).

Here was unquestionably a unique school. Whether it was a
"laboratory" in a really scientific sense is a good question. Here we
must remark the fact that of teaching "media" in the usual sense there
was very little. There was raw material in plenty, clay, wool, lumber, and
so on. It was the pupils who made and grew and raised things. The
school did not simply confront and teach them with the ready-made. It
apparently did not utilize motion pictures, which were in vogue before
Dewey left for Columbia.

The Chicago laboratory school was grounded in and dedicated
to a particular educational philosophy. All in all, it was something different and adjudged good by those who knew it best, pupils, staff, parents, and a corps of university professors who delighted to act as consultants. . . .

MERIAM'S SCHOOL AT MISSOURI

[The school at the University of Missouri] was directed by Junius
Lathrop Meriam. . . . From all accounts the school . . . was an unusual
and bustling one, . . . guaranteed to "terrify the conservative." It was a
school where "subjects" in the ordinary sense were abolished, where
what came to be known as "block-scheduling" replaced the standard
class periods of so many minutes, where something like an advanced

core curriculum with emphasis on personal problems of living was in operation. But if such instructional devices as movies, slides and the newly invented radio of the 1920s were used at this *avant-garde* Missouri school, we have found no record of them.

Of similar schools which were undoubtedly "experimental" as traditional model schools never were, one may read sympathetic descriptions in the Deweys' book (Dewey and Dewey 1920). That they were the heralds of "schools of tomorrow" seems so far to have been an overly optimistic view. For if they scandalized old-line educators, they were also found wanting by those who reverenced not tradition but the canons of science and measurement.

[F. G.] Bonser spoke out strongly, and it would appear with considerable effect, when he was sharply critical of the claims made by many of the new-type experimental schools. He examined eleven of them and charged that on the whole they appraised their work subjectively and philosophically, rather than scientifically. He went on to say, "There is provision for no testing of results in comparison with results from control situations which would afford objective evidence of measurable differences in achievement, if such exist. Both the amount and value of achievements claimed rest upon assertion rather than upon incontrovertible evidence" (Bonser 1926, 361). The laboratory schools at the Universities of Iowa and Chicago and Lincoln School in New York were given a good bill of health. Bonser considered that they "employed the most thoroughgoing scientific procedure" in curricular experimentation (1926, 360).

HORACE MANN–LINCOLN SCHOOL

[At the Lincoln School, which opened in 1917, and at Horace Mann–Lincoln School, which merged with it in 1943], the chief emphasis . . . was on curriculum. Lincoln from the first was to be "a laboratory for the working out of an elementary and secondary curriculum which shall eliminate obsolete material and endeavor to work up in usable form material adapted to the needs of modern living" (Cremin, Shannon, and Townsend 1954, 110). Under a distinguished and devoted staff, a vast amount of curriculum material was developed, tests, workbooks, units, etc. The implications of child development and of social change were considered vitally important in all that was planned and tested.

Visitors came in embarrassing numbers to have a close look at this 6-3-3 laboratory school that was doing away with the obsolete and creating the modern. But somewhere there seemed to be a fatal weakness that prevented Lincoln and the merged Horace Mann–Lincoln School (1944–1947) from having any great influence on school systems throughout the country. The fact that the pupils paid tuition fees and fees that were much more than nominal (from $200 to $300 a year in 1917 and within ten years from $300 to $500) introduced a selective factor not found in the public schools. When one reads that 75 of Lincoln's first 78 graduates went on to college, the selectivity becomes dramatically obvious (Cremin et al. 1954).

In terms of experimentation that was widely applicable, Horace Mann–Lincoln "proved a disappointment" and its fate was definitely sealed when it was a "disappointment financially" as well (Cremin et al. 1954, 235). The doors were closed at the end of the 1947–1948 school year. . . .

Not long after the passing of Horace Mann–Lincoln School there appeared in *Teachers College Record* an article by Dean Hollis L. Caswell which explained the administrative decision. "It was our judgment that a school lacking a normal community setting and with a student body highly selected with regard to intellectual ability, social background, vocational goal, and probable college attendance, held little promise for experimentation of wide significance. . . . Would not experimentation be more significant if undertaken in several schools in cooperation?" (Caswell 1949, 449).

Caswell gave some technical advice to laboratory schools in general by recommending what was then considered to be "experimenting with the provision of an observation room adjoining a (campus school) classroom, with intervening wall constructed of one-way vision glass. Sound connections with the classroom would permit the observer to hear what was said in the classroom but would make it possible to talk in the observation room without being heard in the classroom" (1949, 447). . . .

Caswell deplored the fact that "student teaching was the major purpose served by most campus laboratory schools" in 1949. "The prospective teacher should have experience in situations of the type in which he will have to teach." Moreover, "too great a concentration of student teachers in a school gives it an unreal atmosphere" (1949, 447).

There followed a thoughtful suggestion. "It is quite possible that arrangements that enable the student experiencing difficulty to secure for use in self-analysis a recording, and possibly a motion picture, of a period of work with a group of children, would be a very effective teaching device. Obviously, such equipment would require special arrangements and could not be generally available, but it might be provided in certain classrooms in a campus laboratory school" (1949, 448). If Caswell's suggestion was adopted anywhere we have found no account of it.

EXEUNT NORMAL SCHOOLS

During the years when "experimental schools" like Dewey's and Meriam's and Lincoln were attempting to blaze new trails, the normal schools were being transformed into teachers colleges. For all their limitations, they had created a standard of sorts and done something to develop the concept that teaching could be a profession (Kinney 1964). They had proliferated with a truly wild abandon by 1900, what with those that were state-controlled, those that were under city boards of education, the private ones and an unnumbered host of county institutions. And as if any further complication were needed, more and more colleges and universities throughout the country were coming into the teacher-training field. An era of competition for enrollment had begun. . . .

[But] the great expansion of facilities for teacher education was not accompanied by a corresponding increase in laboratory schools. In the 1840s and 1850s a model school had been considered a *sine qua non* of a normal school. . . . Yet it is a matter of historical fact that the Massachusetts normal schools carried on for some forty years after their model schools were discontinued in the 1850s, largely because they were on "too slender a financial basis." The students simply practiced on one another, a system sometimes described as "playing school, with sham lessons taught to sham classes." But the normal schools neither closed nor apologized for their graduates during the time when the standard demonstration and practice lessons were suspended. . . .

A significant trend . . . was evident by 1885. [Iola Rounds] noted that "out of 233 institutions in the United States offering in some form professional training for teachers, 133 were schools established for some other purpose but having connected with them a normal school department." And "of seventy-five state normal schools in 1885, forty-five did not offer advantages for practical work, while thirty had connected with them a practice department" (Rounds 1885, 582). To bring the record up to date, of some 1,200 institutions in the United States engaged in teacher education in 1964, approximately 205 have campus schools. A slight trend toward an increase in number in the past few years has been reported (Blackmon 1962), but of the long-range tendency there is no question. The important point may be re-emphasized. A campus school is not considered indispensable to a teacher education institution. It seems reasonable to say that it now requires special justification. And for many colleges it is so costly as to be prohibitive (Smith and Johnson 1964). . . .

The transformation from state normal school to state teachers college, started by Ypsilanti, which granted its first B.A. in 1905, proceeded steadily in the first decade of this century, accelerated in the 1920s and was virtually completed in the 1930s. . . . This change, like that of many traditional colleges into teacher-training institutions, was something that "did not occur as the result of any well considered plan," but rather "as a result of struggle for prestige and recognition" (Judd 1933, 47). It would seem beyond question that if some normal schools merely proceeded "with all deliberate speed" to become four-year degree-granting institutions, there were others that showed unseemly haste. But as far as laboratory schools were concerned, there was no discernible increase in their prestige or effectiveness when they became associated with colleges rather than with normal schools. In many of them some anxious attention was given to just what functions they could best perform. And in the twentieth century they were to be critically examined from without. . . .

LABORATORY SCHOOLS AND SURVEYS OF TEACHER EDUCATION

[In studies published between 1920 and 1944, campus schools get scant mention.]

The most ambitious survey of teacher education in the United States was that of the Office of Education, reported in six volumes in 1935. It included a selected bibliography of 1,928 items, reduced from an original 4,000. Of those finally chosen, only fifteen are specific references to "laboratory school" and it is not being overcritical to say that singly and collectively they are disappointing.

One proposal of the report is that "where possible to utilize public affiliated schools for actual practice, it is desirable to make the campus training school largely a laboratory agency for demonstration and experimentation" (Office of Education 1933, III, 97). In the final part of the report we find a sentence whose third word should be noted carefully. "There is slight exaggeration in the statement that there are as many patterns for the use of the training school in the education of teachers as there are institutions in which teachers are prepared" (Office of Education 1933, IV, 123).

An excerpt from one of the report's suggested readings about laboratory schools illustrates typical generalizations in which the literature abounds. "The training-school building should be the best modern public school building in the country. In addition, it should provide the most modern equipment and facilities which are specifically needed for the problem of training teachers" (Johnston 1923, 144). One would welcome a further paragraph, beginning, "For instance."

A Commission on Teacher Education appointed by the American Council on Education had the cooperation of twenty-four teacher education institutions in a study that it reported in 1944. The campus school received only nominal attention, a total of three pages. There was nothing more impressive to record about it than the general introduction of "new teaching aids," unspecified in nature and use, and recently completed arrangements for hot lunches at Prairie View State College in Texas (Armstrong et al. 1944). . . .

PERIODICAL LITERATURE ON THE CAMPUS SCHOOL

The problems and frustrations of the campus school; its common isolation both from the rest of the institution within which it operates and from the institution's service area; the recurring question of what functions it should try to perform; speculations about the future of campus schools and whether they really give promise of becoming centers of experimentation and research; on these and related subjects countless articles have been written over the years. . . . *In toto* they are constructively critical and maintain that laboratory schools are needed. Some of the most severe of them have been written from within the family. It was a former president of a teachers college who hinted darkly at "dry rot" and "senility" in laboratory schools and with no suggestion that they were the rarest of phenomena (Morgan 1946, 168). Just after World War II, he was still hoping, and not too confidently, that some laboratory school would be inspired to "pioneer in the field of experimentation and research" (1946, 168). . . .

[Articles about campus schools are] not particularly helpful in providing promising guidelines for the future. No eager young director of a laboratory school will find in a library of this type of literature anything that can serve as a lamp unto his feet. He will discover a virtual unanimity of opinion that student teaching should not be done on campus, divided opinion on the question of "demonstrations," and a fairly general conviction that much more must be done in unspecified areas of experimentation and research.

PROFESSIONAL ASSOCIATIONS AND THE CAMPUS SCHOOL

At first blush it may seem reasonable to suppose that such important professional literature as the proceedings and meetings of the National Education Association (N.E.A.) and yearbooks like those of the Association for Student Teaching (A.S.T.) and the American Association of Colleges for Teacher Education (A.A.C.T.E.) will be fruitful sources of information about the model school and its successors. This is true if the research interest is about such questions as the proper blend of academic and methods courses, or the value of "demonstration lessons" or the time and the place for student teaching. . . .

During the first thirty years of the N.E.A., the model school was of common interest—but not because of its research achievements or potential. The day of respectable educational research was hardly at the dawn when the model school was a good sixty years old. It was regularly discussed and reported on at annual meetings of the Normal Schools Department of the N.E.A. from the 1870s to 1900. But by the time that professional education had even a modest commitment to real research and experimentation, the model school, by whatever name, was no longer a standard part of more than a small minority of teacher education institutions. So far as the majority were concerned, it was a costly and unnecessary feature, if not an out-and-out anachronism. If the laboratory school stood in need of examination, not to say critical evaluation, the problem could hardly be discussed intelligently, let alone be solved by any representative group of professional educators, 75 percent of whom might have no first-hand experience to draw upon and no prospect of acquiring any.

Two or three of the yearbooks should be mentioned, however. The 34th of the A.S.T. is entitled *Functions of Laboratory Schools in Teacher Education* (Perrodin, 1955). In one of the papers, Lindsey cited contributions that laboratory schools had made to developing the project methods, the unit plan and the core curriculum. But he was obliged to report that "the trend today is for those schools to be used for student teaching, rather than for experimentation" (Lindsey 1955, 62). . . .

The general conclusion of the 1955 A.S.T. annual conference was that observation, demonstration and specialized student teaching were still high on the list of laboratory school functions but it was agreed that research and experimentation were very important, too (Perrodin 1955a). . . .

In its first yearbook, the A.A.C.T.E. came down solidly on the side of research but failed to mention the campus school as a logical place for it (A.A.C.T.E. 1948). By 1957, however, it may have said the final important word on one issue. A discussion group reported a conclusion to which no one objected or demurred. "The campus laboratory school is no longer effective for student teaching. It should be the center for observation, demonstration, and experimentation" (A.A.C.T.E. 1959, 88).

INDIVIDUAL STUDIES AND THESES

The [E. I. F.] Williams study "Actual and Potential Use of Laboratory Schools" . . . was the first reasonably thorough work of its kind. Forty-one states were represented by the 131 training institutions in the sample.

A net conclusion was that "few" laboratory schools were used for experimental purposes. It was apparently beyond the scope of the thesis to give any details. "More institutions, 95.4 percent, used the laboratory school for student teaching than for any other single purpose and an almost equal percentage, 94.5, for observation" (Williams 1942, 217).

[T. M.] Barrington looked closely at 171 teachers colleges and normal schools some ten years after publication of the Williams thesis. He was concerned with the "introduction of selected educational practices into teachers colleges and their laboratory schools." By 1953, moving pictures and radio might have been widely in evidence in teacher education and more particularly in campus schools. The movies are not dealt with, but laboratory schools were found lagging in "radio workshops" to an extent that was "deplorable" (Barrington 1953, 78).

All in all, "teachers colleges and their laboratory schools were discouragingly slow in adopting new educational practices, with the former group of institutions being especially guilty in this respect" (1953, 91). There would seem to have been no startling change in the general situation since Williams gave his attention to it.

In 1955, [L. E.] Bradfield surveyed twenty-four campus elementary schools in seven Southern states and Missouri. He reported that "76 percent of the schools provided for some research and 96 percent provided for at least some experimentation." All twenty-four of the colleges had audio-visual materials "available for use in the campus schools" (1955, 119–120). Lack of detailed information and recourse to "available" impair the value of this investigation.

A 1959 study of thirty-eight laboratory schools connected with universities or teachers colleges, seven of which were visited, the others supplying answers to questionnaires, showed that for the particular sample, "demonstration, observation and participation had occupied so much attention that the success of experimentation was jeopardized" (Hughes 1959, 27). There are repeated references to the necessity for campus schools to do more experimenting and research, but one finds no specific mention of the use of new media, e.g., television, which by 1959 was plainly here to stay.

What appears to have been the most recent study involving a large number of laboratory schools, indeed a majority of them, was the one carried out by [C. R.] Blackmon (1963). And it was concerned exclusively with the "research function."

In the preliminary part of his investigation, Blackmon was in touch with 187 laboratory schools, 140 of which were engaged in some kind of research. The number was then reduced to 125, in forty different states, Puerto Rico and the District of Columbia. Of the 125, twenty-three laboratory schools reported considerable research, and nine of these were finally selected for visitation. . . .

The study reports that in the nine laboratory schools visited, officials who were interviewed "noted that great attention was being given to new techniques, devices and materials, such as teaching machines, team teaching, closed-circuit TV, kinescopes, etc., in relation to both learning theory and the resolving of the mounting pressures of teacher education due to increasing enrollments" (1962, 118). In "at least eight of the nine laboratory schools" research was becoming "increasingly important." Blackmon also found evidence that "much research—particularly 'action research'—had gone unrecorded, unreported, and undisseminated" (1963, 129–131).

In a published abstract of Blackmon's study, two conclusions and a recommendation stand out more sharply than they do in the thesis itself (Blackmon 1963):

Basic research of rigorous design has been neglected in laboratory schools.

Competence in research is becoming a criterion in laboratory school teacher selection.

Laboratory schools should effect research productivity as a hedge against their elimination.

This recommendation seems to mean that laboratory schools should concentrate more on research or run the grave risk of being abolished. . . .

As this chapter was being completed, a doctoral thesis on "The Status and Potential of College Controlled Laboratory Schools" came to hand (White 1964). Its sample was composed of fifty-four schools, more than one-quarter of the total for the nation.

Some eighty percent of the directors are firm in their belief that laboratory schools have more freedom than public schools to engage in experimentation and research. But only about one-third declared that experimentation and research were the major functions of their own schools. Some twenty percent reported no present or recent research.

White could only conclude that "experimentation and research are not among the principal functions of the college-controlled laboratory schools" (1964, 143). He ventured no prediction and saw no trend that justified a stronger statement than "laboratory schools are facing an uncertain future" (1964, 138). . . .

THE EXTREME RECOMMENDATION

Perhaps the sharpest criticism on record of a group of campus schools is that of [H. M.] Brickell. He concluded that those at New York's eleven state university colleges were not experimental and were subject to "powerful restraints that made bold experimentation impossible." They seemed to be wedded to the theory that "the best known methods" should be demonstrated and that untested methods should be left severely alone. Brickell was satisfied that "in the eyes of the public schools, the campus schools are abnormal, artificial, and unreal"

(1961, 51). He granted that they are conveniently located and do provide "readily accessible artificiality." He made one recommendation
about them. They should be closed (1961, 95).

A RIPPLE OR A WAVE?

If the laboratory school of the 1960s can be described by one friendly
writer as "an unresolved problem" (Ohles 1961, 390) and by another as
"searching for identity" (Rzepka 1962, 24) there are at least some signs
. . . that new ground is actually being broken, and on a growing
scale. . . .

Many individual campus schools are known to be taking stock
and planning to do more than give lip-service to experimentation and
research. The one at the University of California, Los Angeles, has gone
on record with a strong statement that leaves no doubt about the direction it will take from now on. It "de-emphasized" practice teaching in
1955, virtually eliminated it by 1960, and then decided that "the
[mission of the] University Elementary School as a laboratory school
in the Department of Education will be experimentation and research
into basic and applied knowledge in the fields of education" (Sherer
1961, 92). . . . "Any observation will be of educational processes and
not of made-to-order demonstrations. . . ." And any "training experiences will necessarily be limited to a few selected students, these to
come from such fields as administration, counseling, curriculum study,
research and teaching" (1961, 95).

Similar stirrings are in evidence in several laboratory schools
throughout the nation. It should not be long until we know whether to
call them a ripple or a wave.

8

Laboratory Schools of the Future

Mina Bayne, Roy Creek, Judith Hechtman,
Crayton L. Buck, John R. Johnson, Bart Tosto, Gregory Ulm,
and Arthur R. King, Jr.

WE HAVE CONCLUDED THIS SERIES OF ESSAYS on university-based laboratory schools in America. We have seen how they responded in times of change; we have discussed their functions; we have looked at the strategic planning processes used by successful schools; we have compared American lab schools with the equivalent Japanese attached schools; we have examined patterns of governance and of finance; we have looked at profiles of some laboratory schools for their patterns of activity; we have reviewed the early history of campus schools.

Now it is time to think of the future. Where should university-based laboratory schools go? What service does the larger field of education and the subset of university-based education require? What are the niches in this larger environment for laboratory schools? Will university-based schools be made redundant by new professional development schools or other specially designated public schools? Is some type of cooperation or division of labor with other types of special schools possible, even recommended? What are some of the necessary conditions for success? This final essay addresses these questions.

THE ENVIRONMENT FOR LABORATORY SCHOOLS

Laboratory schools—indeed all education-related enterprises—find themselves in a period of unusual educational change, with the opportunity for increased service to education. The improvement of education, a perennial issue in America and in most other nations as well, seems to be a concern of everyone—educators and teacher educators, professional unions and their local affiliates, colleges and universities, professional associations, presidents, governors, legislatures, businesses and industries, the armed forces, students at all levels, and the public. Educational consultants, state coordinating agencies, and national governors' conferences have proposed agendas and solutions.

Evidences of this ferment include initiatives by governors and lawmakers, reports and proposals by foundations, commentary by educationists and critics, and the emergence of private educational consulting companies.

The university stake includes the improvement of teacher education, the exploration of alternative models for teacher training and certification, the induction of new teachers into their first positions, staff development, and research and development on a wide variety of topics.

Clearly, there is opportunity for significant service by all well-conceived, well-organized, well-funded, and well-motivated organizations, including university-based laboratory schools.

SOME PROMISING ROLES FOR UNIVERSITY-BASED LABORATORY SCHOOLS

Today's environment presents a rich set of problems, issues, and possibilities.

Educational Technology

We can hardly ignore the potential of electronic classrooms, computer-assisted instruction, video image transfer, satellite communication, networking among local or distant schools, computer simulations, and fax machines, to name a few possibilities for enhancing education through technology.

Yet past promises made for educational technology in both number and intensity must be contrasted to their lack of fulfillment in classrooms. Why have they failed to live up to the claims? Are the basic technologies faulty or inappropriate? Is the development of software the problem? Is training at pre-service and in-service levels the missing link? Is there a shortage of careful evaluative research and curriculum development that can be done in laboratory schools?

A distinctive contribution could be made by a well-resourced, thoroughly evaluated research and development effort. Cooperation and support would be required from the media, industry, federal grants, experimental schools, universities, and industrial training groups. Laboratory schools with their university and school connections may well be proper sites for this effort.

Changes in Curriculum and Instruction

The school curriculum in a dynamic society always requires change. Some changes come through adding new content, some by revitalizing older content, some by adding new elements such as inquiry and critical thinking to perennial subjects, some by presenting content previously reserved for a few to expanded groups of students. The following are a few topics of special promise:

1. Environmental/ecological education is among the topics pressing to be included in the curriculum. Its importance to the community, the nation, and the world needs no argument. Well-conceived and well-developed educational programs will be welcomed. The special capacities of laboratory schools are being used to design and develop programs that integrate scientific, social, and technological knowledge into unified curriculum models. An expanded cooperative interagency effort is recommended.

2. Moral/values education presents an especially difficult educational problem. The tensions of a pluralistic nation, including the perennial and ambiguous heritage of separation of church and state, make this an educational task of great sensitivity. Yet we must not

leave this need unserved. Promising approaches include the development of curriculum-based generic or universal concepts, the
teaching of ethics (one lab school is already experimenting with
an ethics curriculum for high schoolers), sensitively taught classes
in literature and philosophy, comparative religion courses that
meet the canons of objectivity, and the attempt to make values
more explicit in the total educational process.

3. Multicultural education is the sharing of knowledge of and atti-
    tudes toward the different ethnic backgrounds of the students in the
    school, the larger community, and the nation. The curriculum and
    such practices as tracking, which isolates groups from each other in
    classrooms and schools, can be studied, and revised formats for
    education can be developed and evaluated.

    Successful societies converge on the issue of preserving sovereignty
    for the benefit of the whole while tolerating personal and minority
    beliefs. Schools need to address this issue in order that diversity be
    accepted and encouraged, but within the framework of the princi-
    ples of a democratic society that guide responsible behavior.

        Other topics of contemporary interest are inclusion of relevant
Asian and Pacific content, geographical education, global education (a
"middle-aged" idea that needs more work), education for preschoolers,
and education for all students as prospective parents.

At–Risk Students

The schooling of "at-risk" children and youth requires attention.
Included in this broad definition are all who do not finish school
(about 25 percent of students), those who attend but do not receive an
educational program (perhaps another 25 percent or more of the age
group), and those who are making progress in school but have pro-
found personal problems that interfere with their schooling and their
life generally. The demographics of birth and circumstance—low
socioeconomic status, minority ethnicity, one-parent families, dys-
functional families, poorly educated parents, and families that move
from place to place—identify a large proportion of these children.
Among those at risk are youngsters of subcultures that do not easily fit

into the middle-class societal norms that are the standards of the community and the agenda of the schools. This need is especially acute in urban and rural low-income areas.

Selected laboratory schools have strong traditions of work with gifted students and handicapped students in special education programs. The larger group of at-risk children and youth has received less attention. Work is needed to examine the curricular, social, personal, and family variables in educating these students.

Collaborative "Drop–In" Schools

Tied to extended day schools, this model would focus on preventing dropping out. A nontraditional approach to secondary education could include a credit-bearing work-study component. The work-study component would include employment counseling. Since the requirements for high school graduation would be met, tutorial assistance is a necessary element. Such programs can be excellent ways to collaborate with the local school districts, community agencies, state social services, and the criminal justice departments.

Parent Participation in Education

Parents who are eager to participate in the education of their children often lack the wherewithal to do it or believe they lack the skills. Developing an initiative designed to help them achieve success with their children can be a direction for some schools.

Research

Essays in this volume established that research is a dominating and still-growing activity in laboratory schools. Is research the best niche for laboratory schools, with other functions assigned to other special schools? Chapter 2 suggested several research foci to consider in developing a school's work agenda: descriptive, historical, and theoretical studies; case studies and longitudinal studies; experimentation and evaluation; curriculum research and development; and policy research. Distinctive roles for laboratory schools are possible in each of these research forms or some suitable mix.

Alternative Teacher Preparation

The educational literature abounds with rhetoric suggesting that colleges and universities must prepare teachers for the future. But few programmatic approaches have been made to changing what is, in essence, a 1940 model. Laboratory schools should take the initiative in developing pilot programs aimed at preparing teachers whose philosophical outlook and commitment will be to the year 2020 and thereafter.

Teacher Planning, Organization, Leadership, and Management

The processes that successful teachers use—loosely termed management, leadership, planning, and organization—remain difficult to teach to beginners. Are our own theories and approaches adequate to assist in cultivating these processes? Can what is presented in courses and seminars be clearly demonstrated and modeled? If so, can these processes be learned in such a way as to be readily available to the new teacher during practice teaching and the first years of service? Do theories and designs presented to the beginner lead to increased competence of the veteran teacher? Laboratory schools can serve teacher education and the profession generally by designing, developing, and demonstrating better approaches to teaching the theoretical and practical knowledge of teaching.

Schools of Choice and Site–Based Management

Recurrent themes in this decade of reform include "schools of choice" and "school-based management." Laboratory schools, being relatively independent, self-energized schools, have experience in working outside the control of typical school district and state educational structures. They have worked with "volunteer" families and have learned to communicate and serve this clientele. With school-based management becoming a popular form of contemporary school change, the extensive experience of laboratory schools seems valuable. Laboratory schools have experience with many forms of school design, curriculum design and delivery, teaching loads, relationships with parents, relationships with university admissions programs, and administrative and governance systems that can help public schools seeking this type of independence. Laboratory schools can offer empirical and other studies, policy research, internships, workshops, visits to the lab school, and consultative visits to schools.

With the erosion of the traditional family unit comes greater need for making full use of schools. The new educational programs can address the times before and after normal school hours, Saturday schools, and summer schools. The nature, scope, and conditions for schooling are important in establishing the philosophy for these endeavors. Extension of this initiative into teacher preparation and staff development offers great possibilities.

University–Based Laboratory Schools: Their Special Advantages

The university as a base for laboratory schools has been challenged by proposals for locating their perennial and emerging functions into specially designated public schools. Called variously "professional development schools," "key schools," or some other label, these schools are believed by some to have great potential for undertaking necessary teacher education, research and development, and other educational improvement tasks. The Holmes Group of major universities, only a few of which have laboratory schools, has been especially vigorous in espousing this idea. Holmes Group officials have even claimed that "professional development schools will not duplicate yesteryear's university lab schools," apparently believing that university laboratory schools no longer exist (The Holmes Group 1989, 12). One belief is that the university connection taints the work of people associated with these schools, making their products unacceptable to public schools—a belief that laboratory school people find highly inaccurate.

Although the concept of professional development schools differs somewhat from the concept of laboratory schools, the promised accomplishments sound much like the achievements of lab schools. The Holmes Group's call for professional development schools reveals a tacit awareness that universities made a serious mistake when they abolished their laboratory schools a few years back. Teacher educators need laboratories for experimentation and research just as much as professionals in the physical sciences and technologies do.

What case can be made for a university base for special-purpose schools? First, we make the empirical case. Over a hundred laboratory schools now serve elementary and secondary levels; another one hundred or so serve the early education/preschool field. Although their productivity is uneven, many of them make substantial contributions to education. A smaller but still large number have impressive records of achievement.

A campus location and a university base offer clear advantages. Because the key to developing a productive educational laboratory is bringing the academic community and the school community together in common harness, we must either take the university out to selected community schools or bring selected schools into the university community. The latter is by far the more reasonable assumption. University people in education and in the disciplines are pleased to work on school issues and problems, but such work must be compatible with their primary job and must not conflict with their obligations in teaching, working with students, participating in management, and doing research and professional publishing. Few university staff members, especially those with credentials in research and development, can spend more than a limited amount of time away from the campus.

An argument is made that campus schools are unlike "regular" schools—that the campus environment is not typical and that work done in campus schools therefore has little validity for other schools. This argument raises the perennial question whether teachers should learn to use the best knowledge we have—the kind learned in nontypical environments—or whether they should learn only what fits them for a typical environment. Furthermore, the question holds equally for alternatives such as professional development schools, which are bound to differ from typical schools in mission, in resources, in facilities, and in selection of staff.

Universities offer many special features and services that experimental schools find essential. They have the freedom and backing to experiment; they have contact with like-minded institutions; they have ready access to a large array of intellectual and professional resources, including easy access to libraries and information networks; they have flexible employment systems for short-term and part-time employees; they have the support of research administrators; they have staffs and facilities to support research and development; they can grant credits and degrees in support of training and staff development; they have the use of revolving funds for recovering the costs of reports and curriculum materials; their salary schedules can be more readily based on accomplishment and responsibility in a range of specialties than those in regular schools; they exist in an environment that attracts research-oriented professionals; and they regularly mount exchange programs with institutions throughout the world. Staffs of university schools can more readily be woven into teacher education, graduate study, and other attractive types of service. As participants in university governance, they can influence university policy and procedure.

University schools usually have flexibility, immunity from rule-setting boards and bureaucracies, and the encouragement to take unusual risks. Parents who send students to university schools accept a program tailored to the larger needs of education, not solely to the benefit of their students, recognizing that the two go hand in hand. Parents in public schools are less likely to understand and accept such conditions.

RELATING TO OTHER SPECIAL–PURPOSE SCHOOLS

University-based laboratory schools cannot possibly provide to universities all the services that require school facilities, personnel, and programs. There are too many teachers and other professionals to be prepared, too much research and development to be accomplished, and too much in-service education to be provided.

Hence the issue is not whether we ought to have either university-based schools or special-purpose public schools; the question is rather how many of each type we need to do what work. One can imagine a wide set of affiliations or partnerships being formed. We already have partnerships of universities and public schools sharing responsibilities, facilities, and staffs, to the benefit of both. Partnerships of laboratory schools in common enterprise have been noted in this book.

This open, flexible approach to sponsoring special-purpose schools is attractive in that it prevents premature decisions on what types of schools are the most effective for what. Experience is a great teacher, an essential testing ground of ideas and assumptions. We should mount and fund a variety of special schools and keep our long-term options open.

THE CONDITIONS OF FUTURE SUCCESS FOR LABORATORY SCHOOLS

Conditions for the success of laboratory schools in the future fall into three categories:

- the role or niche of the laboratory school
- the structure, operations, and resources of the laboratory school
- the need for visibility and recognition of work done in the laboratory school

The Role or Niche of the Laboratory School

The earlier essays presented a variety of programs for and approaches to important educational service. Because potential niches are almost without limit, each school must find roles that are valued by its constituents—university colleagues and administrators, school staffs, educational authorities, and governmental and legislative bodies. The roles accepted by each school must be within its capability for satisfactory fulfillment, including its present and probable resources.

As we noted earlier, laboratory schools co-exist with other special-purpose schools and educational organizations that do, or could do, similar kinds of work: regional laboratories, teacher service centers, colleges of education, private service organizations, and professional development schools among them. Laboratory schools must mount programs that are distinctive but inadequately served by other institutions. Collaborative relationships with these other organizations extend the influence of all participants. The successful school will resist the temptation to be all things to all people, especially to undertake incompatible kinds of work.

The Structure, Operations, and Resources of the Laboratory School

The laboratory school must have the structure, operations, and resources to deliver on its commitments. Staff, of course, is the primary resource. The experience of laboratory schools is that unusual roles require unusual people. It is not easy to convert a person from one role—say teaching third grade or American history—to some other professional role. As one moves away from the typical role of teaching to less typical roles in research, writing, staff development, team leadership, and the like, the potential for a successful professional role change becomes increasingly problematic. For example, a well-staffed laboratory school engaged in curriculum research and development has specialists in curriculum theory, instructional design, evaluation, editing, publishing, dissemination (including marketing), and management of a small business. Even very good classroom teachers cannot convert to these roles without selective screening, demonstrated interest and commitment, career development, and years of growth in a supportive environment. Modified job loads are usually required. For example, it has been found that an educator engaged in curriculum research and writing must have a light teaching load (no more than one or two hours a day) and a support staff in relevant specialties.

Leadership is as important to laboratory schools as it is to any organization that attempts to work creatively with complex human problems. The successful leader brings a special set of capacities: thorough knowledge, theoretical and practical, of education; skill in bringing diverse individuals and specializations into working teams; ability to communicate well with the school's constituents; and the capacity to engage in strategic planning in the school's complex environment.

The school must create a network of organizations that will support and enhance its work. First, the quality of product is improved through shared insights, strengths, and resources. Second, an organization that is connected in many ways has greater survival potential than one with few or no institutional connections.

The Need for Visibility and Recognition of Work Done in the Laboratory School

Laboratory schools must get visibility and recognition. The professional and public media produce a huge quantity of material on educational improvement—its promises, its problems, its needs, its cures. They are easily squeezed out by advertised programs that are new, simple, popular (the bandwagon effect), and aggressively promoted. Because laboratory schools and their programs are none of these, their stories get told neither often nor well. The major responsibility for securing visibility and recognition lies with laboratory school people themselves, especially their leaders and their professional organizations.

CONCLUSION

These essays on university-based laboratory schools have reflected the experience of their leaders during the past twenty years. These decades have been a time of consolidation for the laboratory school movement in America, which followed the tumultuous period of the 1950s and 1960s when sixty-five schools were eliminated. Consolidation took many forms. Some schools persevered in the traditional role of demonstration and practice teaching, often weaving them into a broader set of services coming to be called clinical practice. A larger group undertook new roles in research, in development, in in-service training, and in serving newer types of clients—the handicapped or the gifted. Some schools found support and expanded roles by tying themselves to public schools. Others have formulated programs with networks of other laboratory schools.

A useful and necessary nationwide dialogue has been maintained by the National Association of Laboratory Schools. The association sponsors regional meetings of laboratory school staffs, holds an annual meeting in conjunction with the American Association of Colleges of Teacher Education, and publishes the *National Association of Laboratory Schools Journal.*

As we complete this book, we note the nationwide demand for educational improvement—a demand that requires responses from all elements in the nation's education-related institutions. The innovative and the competent will capitalize on this opportunity. We believe that schools built on a university base have the heritage, the experience, and the leadership to be among the agencies that can raise the level of service to the teaching profession.

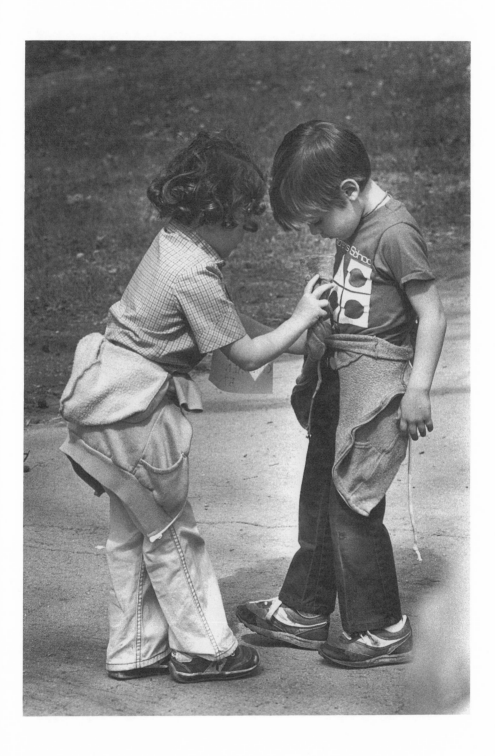

Comprehensive Bibliography
about Laboratory Schools

Abrams, P. (1971). Crisis in the lab school. *Laboratory School Administrators Association Newsletter, 13* (1), 50–63.

Acheson, K., & Olivero, J. L. (1970). Educational laboratories and teacher education. *Journal of Teacher Education, 21,* 330–331.

Adams, W. H. (1950). Pushbutton observation for student teaching. *Texas Outlook, 34* (1), 26–27.

Albrecht, J. E. (1982, Fall). Of power, vultures, and lab schools. *National Association of Laboratory Schools Journal, 7* (2), 1–9.

American Association of Colleges for Teacher Education. (1948). *First yearbook.* Washington, DC: the Association.

American Association of Colleges for Teacher Education. (1959). *Teacher education for the future: Twelfth yearbook.* Washington, DC: the Association.

American Association of Teachers Colleges. (1926). *Standards for accrediting teachers colleges.* Oneonta, NY: the Association.

American Council on Education. (1938). *Major issues in teacher education.* Washington, DC: the Council.

American Council on Education. (1946). *The improvement of teacher education*. Washington, DC: the Council.

Armstrong, W. E., Hollis, E. V., & Davis, H. E. (1944). *The college and teacher education*. Washington, DC: American Council on Education.

Ashmore, H. L. (1951). An evaluation of state-supported campus laboratory schools in selected southeastern states. *Educational Administration and Supervision, 37*, 80–97.

Association for Student Teaching. (1964). *New developments, research, and experimentation in professional laboratory experiences*. (AST Bulletin No. 22). Cedar Falls, IA: the Association.

Barker, S. L. (1985, Winter). Balancing needs and enrollment—The role of the lottery. *National Association of Laboratory Schools Journal, 9* (4), 48–50.

Barnard, H. (1839, June). First annual report to the secretary of the board of commissioners of the common schools of Connecticut. *Connecticut Common School Journal, 1*, 174.

Barnard, H. (1851). *On normal schools*. Hartford: Case, Tiffany and Co. (Reprint by Colorado State Teachers College, 1929)

Barrington, T. M. (1953). *The introduction of selected educational practices into teachers colleges and their laboratory schools*. New York: Bureau of Publications, Teachers College, Columbia University.

Beberman, M. (1968, Spring). The role of laboratory schools in curriculum development. *Laboratory School Administrators Association Newsletter, 10* (3).

Behling, H. E., Jr. (1966, Winter). Role perceptions of laboratory schools. *Laboratory School Administrators Association Newsletter, 9* (2), 15. (Reprinted in C. R. Blackmon (Ed.), 1970, *Laboratory schools, U.S.A.—Studies and readings* (Southwestern Studies: Humanities Series, No. 3, pp. 151–153).

Lafayette: University of Southwestern Louisiana. (ERIC Document Reproduction Service No. ED 045 569))

Bell, H. (1971). Secondary participation: Prelude to student teaching. *Supervisors' Quarterly, 6* (3), 3–6.

Berliner, D. C. (1985). Laboratory settings and the study of teacher education. *Journal of Teacher Education, 36* (6), 2–8.

Bigelow, K. W. (1974). An account of the passing of the teachers college. In S. Cohen (Ed.), *Education in the United States: A documentary history.* (Vol. 5, pp. 2676–2679). New York: Random House.

Bixby, P. W., & Mitzel, H. E. (Eds). (1965). *Campus school to a research and dissemination center* (NDEA Report No. VII B–374). University Park: College of Education, Pennsylvania State University. (ERIC Document Reproduction Service No. ED 003 774)

Blackmon, C. R. (1963). The research function in selected college-controlled laboratory schools. *Dissertation Abstracts, 23,* 2766. (University Microfilms No. 63–2655) (An extended abstract in C. R. Blackmon (Ed.), 1970, *Laboratory schools, U.S.A.— Studies and readings* (Southwestern Studies: Humanities Series, No. 3, pp. 86–96). Lafayette: University of Southwestern Louisiana. (ERIC Document Reproduction Service No. ED 045 569)

Blackmon, C. R. (1964). The research function in selected college-controlled laboratory schools. In Association for Student Teaching, *New developments, research, and experimentation in professional laboratory experiences* (AST Bulletin No. 22, pp. 127–129). Cedar Falls, IA: the Association.

Blackmon, C. R. (Ed.). (1970). *Laboratory schools, U.S.A.—Studies and readings.* (Southwestern Studies: Humanities Series, No. 3). Lafayette: University of Southwestern Louisiana. (ERIC Document Reproduction Service No. ED 045 569)

Blackmon, C. R. (1970). The present and future status of the college-controlled laboratory school. In C. R. Blackmon (Ed.), *Laboratory schools, U.S.A.—Studies and readings* (Southwestern Studies: Humanities Series, No. 3, pp. 64–85). Lafayette: University of Southwestern Louisiana. (ERIC Document Reproduction Service No. ED 045 569)

Blackmon, C. R. (1975, October). The campus laboratory school as a necessary facility for quality teacher education. *National Association of Laboratory Schools Newsletter,* pp. 11–18.

Blackmon, C. R., & McDuffie, J. L. (1980, Winter). Laboratory schools and college special education departments performing below potential for collaboration with each other and local education agencies on Public Law 94–142. *National Association of Laboratory Schools Journal,* pp. 13–20.

Blair, L. C., Curtis, D. E., & Moon, A. C. (1958). *The purposes, functions, and uniqueness of the college-controlled laboratory school* (AST Bulletin No. 9). Cedar Falls, IA: Association for Student Teaching.

Bolton, F. E. (1900). Original investigation in normal schools. *Education, 20,* 548–556, 601–612.

Bonser, F. G. (1926). *Curriculum-making in laboratory schools: Twenty-sixth yearbook of the National Society of the Study of Education* (Part I). Bloomington IL: Public School Publishing Co.

Bowman, D. (1973, June). Commitment: The dean's role. *Laboratory School Administators Association Newsletter, 14* (3), 14–38.

Boyden, A. C. (1933). *The history of Bridgewater Normal School.* Bridgewater, MA: Bridgewater Normal Alumni Association.

Braddock, C. (1968). What's going on in the lab schools? *Southern Education Report, 3,* 3–7.

Bradfield, L. E. (1955). A survey of twenty-four campus elementary schools. *Journal of Teacher Education, 6,* 118–121.

Brazee, E. N. (1980, Winter). Laboratory schools: Don't wait for someone else to lead. *National Association of Laboratory Schools Journal*, pp. 40–42.

Brickell, H. M. (1961). *Organizing New York State for educational change*. Albany: State Education Department.

Broudy, H. S. (1985). Variations in search of a theme. *Journal of Educational Thought, 19*, 34–39.

Brubacher, J. S. (1960). Teacher education—Development. In C. W. Harris (Ed.), *Encyclopedia of Educational Research* (3rd ed., pp. 1452–1454). New York: Macmillan.

Bryan, R. C. (1961). The vital role of the campus school. *Journal of Teacher Education, 12*, 275–281.

Buck, C. L. (1971). *Campus school self study*. (Unpublished, available from author, Oswego, NY)

Buck, C. L. (1975, May). Sentence first—Verdict pending. *National Association of Laboratory Schools Newsletter*, pp. 14–25.

Buck, C. L. (1976). Phaseout narrowly averted. *National Association of Laboratory Schools Journal, 1* (1).

Buck, C. L. (1978). Inservice education for teachers of gifted/talented students. *National Association of Laboratory Schools Journal, 3* (2).

Bucklen, H. E. (1952). The campus school—What are its functions? *Journal of Teacher Education, 3*, 201–203.

Cappa, D. (1972). College-controlled laboratory schools. *Improving College and University Teaching, 20*, 110–111.

Cardinell, C. F. (1978, May 3). New paths for America's laboratory schools. Paper presented at the School of Education, Indiana State University. (ERIC Document Reproduction Service No. ED 153 997)

Carnegie Foundation for the Advancement of Teaching. (1974). The move to transform normal schools into colleges (1912). In S. Cohen (Ed.), *Education in the United States: A Documentary History* (Vol. 5, pp. 2670–2672). New York: Random House. (Reprinted from *Seventh annual report of the Carnegie Foundation for the Advancement of Teaching,* 1912, New York, pp. 149–152)

Carrington, J. W. (1942). Functions of laboratory schools without student teachers. In Association for Student Teaching, *Twenty-first annual yearbook* (pp. 61–69). Lock Haven, PA: the Association.

Caswell, H. L. (1949). The place of the campus laboratory school in the education of teachers. *Teachers College Record, 50,* 441–450.

Chaloupka, D. (1967, Spring). Self-evaluation: A preliminary exploration for laboratory schools. *Laboratory School Administrators Association Newsletter, 9* (3), 20–30.

Chase, F. S. (1980). The Chicago Laboratory Schools: Retrospect and prospect. *UCLA Educator, 21* (2), 38–44.

Cierpilowski, G., & Zimmerman, E. (1975, May). An interagency cooperative project. *National Association of Laboratory Schools Newsletter, 1,* 54–62.

Class of 1938. (1938). *Were we guinea pigs?* New York: Henry Holt.

Cloyd, A. (1946). The campus school in relation to emerging patterns of educational theory and practice. *Peabody Journal of Education, 23,* 274–276.

Colvin, C. M. (1981, Spring). Golightly Center: A partnership in urban education. *National Association of Laboratory Schools Journal,* pp. 18–19.

Congreve, W. (1967, Spring). Every school a lab school. *Laboratory School Administrators Association Newsletter, 9* (3), 10–19.

Copeland, W. D. (1982). Laboratory experiences in teacher education. In H. E. Mitzel (Ed.), *Encyclopedia of educational research* (5th ed., pp. 1008–1019). New York: Macmillan.

Cornthwaite, D. L. (1972). *Defining the role and functions of campus laboratory schools for the decade of the seventies through an investigation of studies of laboratory schools completed between 1965 and 1970.* Unpublished doctoral dissertation, George Washington University.

Creek, R. J. (1979, November). Those long-range goals and how to achieve them. *National Association of Laboratory Schools Journal,* pp. 25–26.

Creek, R. J. (1984). The educational laboratory of the future. *National Association of Laboratory Schools Journal, 9* (2), 47–53.

Creek, R. J. (1990, Winter). Human subjects protection: Guidelines for laboratory schools. *National Association of Laboratory Schools Journal, 14* (2), 14–21.

Cremin, L. A. (1961). *The transformation of the school.* New York: Knopf.

Cremin, L. A. (1976). *Public education.* New York: Basic Books.

Cremin, L. A., Shannon, D. A., & Townsend, M. E. (1954). *A history of Teachers College, Columbia University.* New York: Columbia University Press.

Cubberly, E. P. (1920). *The history of education.* New York: Houghton Mifflin.

Cubberly, E. P. (1934). *Public education in the United States.* New York: Houghton Mifflin.

Cyphert, F. (1963). Contributions a laboratory school could make to the professional sequence. *Laboratory School Administrators Association Newsletter, 6* (1).

Deer, G. H. (1946). The laboratory school as a carrier of educational philosophy. *Peabody Journal of Education, 23,* 279–282.

De Graff, E. V., & Smith, M. K. (1884). *Development lessons for teachers.* New York: Lovell.

Demos, E. S. (1990, Winter). Functions of laboratory schools (collaboration & networking). *National Association of Laboratory Schools Journal, 14* (2), 34–39.

De Pencier, I. B. (1967). *The history of the laboratory schools: The University of Chicago.* Chicago: Quadrangle Books. (Original work published 1960)

Dewey, J. (1896). The university school. *University Record, 1,* 417–422.

Dewey, J. (1904). The relation of theory to practice in education. In C. A. McMurry (Ed.), *The relation of theory to practice in the education of teachers: The third yearbook of the National Society for the Study of Education* (Part I). Bloomington, IL: Public School Publishing Co.

Dewey, J. (1952). Introduction. In E. R. Clapp, *The use of resources in education.* New York: Harper & Brothers.

Dewey, J. (1956). *The child and the curriculum, The school and society.* Chicago: Phoenix Books, University of Chicago Press. (Original works published 1902 and 1900, respectively)

Dewey, J. (1965). The theory of the Chicago experiment. In K. C. Mayhew & A. C. Edwards, *The Dewey School.* New York: Atheling. (Original work published 1936)

Dewey, J. (1972). *The early works of John Dewey* (Vol. 5, 1895–1898). Carbondale: Southern Illinois University Press.

Dewey, J., & Dewey, E. (1915). *Schools of tomorrow.* New York: Dutton.

Dinger, J. C. (1972). The creative use of laboratory schools in preparing special education teachers. *Education and Training of the Mentally Retarded, 7* (4), 194–196.

Driscoll, R. L., & Wheeler, D. (1979). *Teacher education center—A displaced campus school?* (ERIC Document Reproduction Service No. ED 182 298)

Duea, J. M. (1976). *An assessment of provisions for practical teacher education experiences and research in public, private, and laboratory schools.* Unpublished doctoral dissertation, Iowa State University.

Duea, J. M. (1980, Spring). Employment, tenure and promotion practices in laboratory schools. *National Association of Laboratory Schools Journal,* pp. 48–62.

Duea, J. M., Jester, J., Tobin, W., & Weller, D. (1982). Laboratory schools *do* make a difference. *National Association of Laboratory Schools Journal,* 7 (1), 1–3.

Durkin, L. (1979, June). The cooperating laboratory school: An integral part of the competency based teacher education program. *National Association of Laboratory Schools Journal,* pp. 27–28.

Edwards, A. C. (1965). The evolution of Mr. Dewey's principles of education. In K. C. Mayhew & A. C. Edwards, *The Dewey School.* New York: Atheling. (Original work published 1936)

Elementary School Teacher. (1903). *3* (10), 661–717. (Issue devoted to University of Chicago Laboratory School)

Elsbree, W. S. (1939). *The American teacher.* New York: American Book Co.

El–Shibiny, M. E. M. (1951). *A proposition for redesigning the functional role of the modern laboratory school: A study of the implications of the philosophical, psychological and aesthetic factors for the curriculum organization.* Unpublished doctoral dissertation, Ohio State University.

Eubank, L. A. (1931, April). The organization and administration of laboratory schools in state teachers colleges. *Northeast Missouri State Teachers College Bulletin, 31,* 73–75.

Fleming, J. N. (1970). The jointly-sponsored city school system–university laboratory school: Advantages and problems. In C. R. Blackmon (Ed.), *Laboratory schools, U.S.A.—Studies and readings* (Southwestern Studies: Humanities Series, No. 3, pp. 154–169). Lafayette: University of Southwestern Louisiana. (ERIC Document Reproduction Service No. ED 045 569)

Florida, Department of Education. (1976). *Evaluation of state university laboratory schools.* Tallahassee: Florida State Department of Education. (ERIC Document Reproduction Service No. ED 131 034)

Florida, Department of Education. (1976). *Study of state coordination of research and development efforts for education.* Tallahassee: Florida State Department of Education. (ERIC Document Reproduction Service No. ED 131 035)

Flowers, J., & others. (1948). *School and community laboratory experiences in teacher education.* Oneonta, NY: Committee on Standards and Surveys, American Association of Teachers Colleges.

Fossieck, T. H. (1965, Spring). The laboratory school's influence on the educational community. *Laboratory School Administrators Association Newsletter, 7* (4), 21–25.

Francis, T. J. (1949). *Cooperative coordination of the laboratory school and other departments of a teachers college* (Report of a Type C Project). New York: Teachers College, Columbia University.

Frantz, M. L. (1959). *An analysis of professional laboratory experiences provided prior to student teaching for students preparing to be secondary school teachers.* Unpublished doctoral dissertation, Teachers College, University of Nebraska.

Frazier, A. (1958). How can laboratory schools work together to fulfill their roles? In *The role of the laboratory school in teacher education* (Proceedings of a Conference held at the P. K. Yonge Laboratory School, November 23–25, pp. 26–32). Gainesville: College of Education, University of Florida.

Fremdling, E. (1974). Teacher education at the university elementary school, UCLA. *UCLA Educator, 16* (2), 21–22.

Friedman, M. A., Brinlee, P. S., & Hayes, P. (1980). *Improving teacher education: Resources and recommendations.* New York: Longman.

Frisbie, K. G. (1975, October). A concept for changing the University of Northern Colorado Laboratory School to a learning center funded as a state-wide school district. *National Association of Laboratory Schools Newsletter,* pp. 34–43.

Frisbie, K. G. (1978, October). The role of the University of Northern Colorado Laboratory School in the professional teacher education program. *National Association of Laboratory Schools Journal,* pp. 27–43.

Fristoe, D. (1942). Early beginnings of laboratory schools. *Educational Administration and Supervision, 28,* 219–223.

Fritz, M. K. (1985). The state normal schools: Teaching teachers and others. *Pennsylvania Heritage, 11* (4).

Garner, W. L., Jr. (1986). To be or not to be? What does a lab school do? *National Association of Laboratory Schools Journal, 10* (3), 16–19.

Gaskill, A. R., & Carlson, A. A. (1958). Is the campus laboratory school obsolescent? *School and Society, 86,* 106–107. (Reprinted in C. R. Blackmon (Ed.), 1970, *Laboratory Schools, U.S.A.— Studies and Readings* (Southwestern Studies: Humanities Series, No. 3, pp. 170–174). Lafayette: University of Southwestern Louisiana. (ERIC Document Reproduction Service No. ED 045 569))

Giffin, W. M. (1906). *School days in the fifties* (to which is appended an autobiographical sketch of Francis Wayland Parker). Chicago: Flanagan.

Glennon, V. J. (1957). *The road ahead in teacher education: The 1957 J. Richard Street Lecture.* Syracuse, NY: Syracuse University Press.

Good, H. G. (1960). *A history of western education.* New York: Macmillan. (pp. 445–450)

Goodlad, J. I. (1971, May). The role of laboratory schools in innovation and experimentation. *National Association of Laboratory Schools Newsletter, 13,* 31–49.

Goodlad, J. I. (1980). How laboratory schools go awry. *UCLA Educator, 21* (2), 46–53.

Greenblatt, B., & Eberhard, L. (1973). *Children on campus: A survey of pre-kindergarten programs at institutions of higher education in the United States.* Buffalo: State University of New York Research Foundation. (ERIC Document Reproduction Service No. ED 088 608)

Haberman, M. (1985). Fifty-one predictions regarding teacher education. *Teacher Education and Practice, 2* (1), 57–60.

Haimbach, D. (1959). *A study of the functions and practices of the P. K. Yonge Laboratory School.* Unpublished doctoral dissertation, College of Education, University of Florida.

Hearn, R. E. (1974, May). Research as a function of selected college-controlled laboratory schools. *Laboratory School Administrators Association Newsletter, 15,* 44–63.

Hendrick, I. G. (1980). University controlled laboratory schools in historical perspective. *UCLA Educator, 21* (2), 54–60.

Hicks, R. D., & Monroe, E. E. (1982, Winter). The laboratory school and teacher education interdepartmental involvement. *National Association of Laboratory Schools Journal,* pp. 10–13.

Himmelman, F. M. (1954). *A survey of the status, policies and practices of the campus schools at the nine Wisconsin state colleges*. Unpublished doctoral dissertation, School of Education, Northwestern University.

Hodges, J. B. (1977). *Research and diffusion process: K. P. Yonge Laboratory School*. Gainesville: University of Florida.

Hodges, J. B., & Fox, J. N. (1974, May). The laboratory school as a force for change in education. *Laboratory School Administrators Association Newsletter, 15*, 8–26.

Holbrook, A. (1860). *The normal*. New York: Barnes and Burr.

Holland, E. O. (1912). *The Pennsylvania state normal schools and public school system* (Contributions to Education, No. 55) New York: Teachers College, Columbia University.

The Holmes Group. (1989). *Work in progress: The Holmes Group one year on*. East Lansing, MI: Holmes Group.

Howd, M. C. (1964, Winter). The future of the laboratory school. *Laboratory School Administrators Association Newsletter, 6* (3), 5–8. (Reprinted in C. R. Blackmon (Ed.), 1970, *Laboratory schools, U.S.A.—Studies and readings* (Southwestern Studies: Humanities Series, No. 3, pp. 54–63). Lafayette: University of Southwestern Louisiana. (ERIC Document Reproduction Service No. ED 045 569))

Howd, M. C. (1970). Survey of laboratory schools in the United States—1964. In C. R. Blackmon (Ed.), *Laboratory schools, U.S.A.—Studies and readings* (Southwestern Studies: Humanities Series, No. 3, pp. 174–191). Lafayette: University of Southwestern Louisiana. (ERIC Document Reproduction Service No. ED 045 569)

Howd, M. C., & Browne, K. A. (1970). *National survey of campus laboratory schools—1969*. Washington, DC: American Association of Colleges for Teacher Education. (ERIC Document Reproduction Service No. ED 036 490)

Hoye, A. G. (1969). Progress report: Marshall University High School. *Laboratory School Administrators Association Newsletter, 11* (3).

Hughes, O. (1959). The role of the campus laboratory school. *Bulletin of the Indiana University School of Education, 35* (2), 1–48.

Hunsucker, F. (1957, March). The council on professional laboratory experiences. *Teachers College Journal, 28,* 74–79.

Hunter, M. (1970). Expanding roles of laboratory schools. *Phi Delta Kappan, 52,* 14–19.

Hunter, M. (1971). Why is a laboratory school? *Instructor, 80* (10), 58–60.

Hutton, H. (1965). Historical background of the campus school in America. In P. W. Bixby & H. E. Mitzel (Eds.), *Campus school to a research and dissemination center* (pp. 1–57). University Park: Pennsylvania State University. (ERIC Document Reproduction Service No. ED 003 774)

Hymer, R. C. (1974, November). Laboratory schools: A vital force in American education. *Laboratory School Administrators Association Newsletter, 15,* 1–2.

Jackson, J. B. (1967). An evaluation of the relative importance of the various functions performed by a campus laboratory school. *Journal of Teacher Education, 18,* 293–303.

Jackson, C. L., & Achilles, C. M. (1988). The lab school revisited. *National Forum of Applied Educational Research Journal, 1* (2).

Jaggers, C. H. (1946). The functions of the laboratory school. *Peabody Journal of Education, 23,* 276–279.

Jarman, A. M. (1932). *The administration of laboratory schools: A study of laboratory schools connected with departments, schools and colleges of education in state universities.* Ann Arbor, MI: George Wahr.

Jeffers, G. C., Michalak, D. A., & Williams, B. L. (1981, Spring). Teacher education in transition. *National Association of Laboratory Schools Journal*, p. 12.

Johnson, J. (1968). *A brief history of student teaching*. De Kalb, IL: Creative Educational Publishing.

Johnson, J. R. (1987). [National Association of Laboratory Schools survey]. Unpublished raw data. Available from author at Indiana University of Pennsylvania, Indiana, PA.

Johnson, S. O., & Franklin, H. (1980, January). Role transformation for laboratory schools: A joint effort. *National Association of Laboratory Schools Journal*, *5*.

Johnston, L. M. (1923). The training school building a factor in teacher training. *Educational Administration and Supervision*, *9*, 139–145.

Judd, C. H. (1925). The influence of scientific studies in education on teacher training institutions. *Peabody Journal of Education*, *11*, 291–300.

Judd, C. H. (1933). *Problems of education in the United States*. New York: McGraw–Hill.

Judd, C. H., & Parker, S. C. (1916). *Problems involved in standardizing state normal schools*. (Bureau of Education Bulletin No. 12). Washington, DC: Bureau of Education.

Kasnic, M. J. (1986). University and public school collaboration: Keeping a laboratory school open. *National Association of Laboratory Schools Journal*, *11* (1), 33–39.

Keislar, E. R. (1980). The inquiry-oriented laboratory school. *UCLA Educator*, *21* (2), 26–31.

Kelley, E. H. (1964). *College-controlled laboratory schools in the United States—1964*. Washington, DC: American Association of Colleges for Teacher Education. (ERIC Document Reproduction Service No. ED 025 449)

Kelley, E. H. (1964). Some pertinent facts concerning the campus laboratory school in the United States. In Association for Student Teaching, *New developments, research, and experimentation in professional laboratory experiences* (AST Bulletin No. 22, pp. 141–144). Cedar Falls, IA: the Association.

Kelley, E. H. (1967). *The status of the campus laboratory school in the United States.* Unpublished doctoral dissertation, Indiana University. (Excerpted in Fall 1967 *Laboratory School Administrators Association Newsletter, 10* (1))

Kelley, E. H. (1970). Brief histories of the Laboratory School Administrators Associations. In C. R. Blackmon (Ed.), *Laboratory schools, U.S.A.—Studies and readings* (Southwestern Studies: Humanities Series, No. 3, pp. 192–195). Lafayette: University of Southwestern Louisiana. (ERIC Document Reproduction Service No. ED 045 569)

Kelley, E. H. (1970). The historical development of the campus laboratory school. In C. R. Blackmon (Ed.), *Laboratory schools, U.S.A.—Studies and readings* (Southwestern Studies: Humanities Series, No. 3, pp. 4–35). Lafayette: University of Southwestern Louisiana. (ERIC Document Reproduction Service No. ED 045 569)

King, A. R., Jr. (1987). Challenge to laboratory schools: Finding a niche. In *National Association of Laboratory Schools Eminent Educator Lecture Series* (Vol. 1, pp.1–13). Buffalo, NY: National Association of Laboratory Schools.

King, A. R., Jr. (in press). The University Laboratory School at the University of Hawaii (U.S.A.): A center for developmental research in curriculum. In B. Möller (Ed.), *The logics of education: Education as an interdisciplinary subject.* Germany: Universität Oldenburgh.

King, A. R., Jr., & Mizoue, Y. (1990). Laboratory schools in Japan and the United States: A comparison. *Pacific–Asian Education, 2* (1), 33–40.

Kinney, L. B. (1964). *Certification in education.* Englewood Cliffs, NJ: Prentice–Hall.

Kohn, D. A., & Turner, R. J. (1968). The University of Missouri Laboratory School and Office of Instructional Television Co-operative Program: A description. *Laboratory School Administrators Association Newsletter, 10* (3).

Koopman, M. (1944). A laboratory school evaluates its contributions to teacher education. *Educational Research Bulletin of Ohio State University, 23,* 7–13.

Kowalski, T. J. (1986). Modeling instruction: The role of laboratory schools. *National Association of Laboratory Schools Journal, 10* (3), 11–15.

Krause, D. L. (1977). The laboratory school in an R&D setting. *Educational Perspectives: Journal of the College of Education of the University of Hawaii, 16* (2), 23–25.

Krause, D. L. (1978, May). From a campus laboratory school to an R&D center. *National Association of Laboratory Schools Journal, 3.* (ERIC Document Reproduction Service No. ED 160 603)

Kuschman, W. (1970). Let's talk sense about laboratory schools. *Clearing House, 45* (1), 56.

Lamb, P. M. (1960). *An investigation of educational research in selected elementary laboratory schools.* Unpublished doctoral dissertation, Ohio State University.

Lamb, P. M. (1962). The laboratory school: An historical perspective. *Journal of Educational Research, 56,* 107–109.

Landreth, C. (1964). Child development laboratories on university campuses. *Child Development, 35,* 989–992.

Lang, D. C. (1957). *An analysis of the campus secondary schools maintained by public institutions.* Unpublished doctoral dissertation, Teachers College, University of Nebraska.

Lang, D. C. (1959). Current theory and practice in connection with the function of the campus laboratory school. *Educational Administration and Supervision, 45,* 36–43.

Larson, A. H. (1942). Function of secondary training school in education. *Educational Administration and Supervision, 28,* 65–68.

Lathrop, R. L., & Beal, D. K. (1965). Current status of selected college-related schools. In P. W. Bixby & H. E. Mitzel (Eds.), *Campus school to a research and dissemination center* (NDEA Report No. VII B–374, pp. 72–96). University Park: Pennsylvania State University. (ERIC Document Reproduction Service No. ED 003 774)

Legislative hearing on continuing New Jersey laboratory schools. (1969). *Laboratory School Administrators Association Newsletter, 11* (3).

Lindsey, M. (1954). Standard VI—Five Years After. In *Seventh yearbook of the American Association of Colleges for Teacher Education* (pp. 112–133). Oneonta, NY: the Association.

Lindsey, M. (1969). *Annotated bibliography on the professional education of teachers.* Washington, DC: Association for Student Teaching.

Lindsey, T. (1955). The use of laboratory schools as facilities for research and experimentation. In A. Perrodin (Ed.), *Functions of laboratory schools in teacher education: Thirty-fourth yearbook—1955* (pp. 61–78). Lock Haven, PA: Association for Student Teaching.

Lloyd, F. V., Jr. (1965, Spring). But you are a *lab* school. *Laboratory School Administrators Association Newsletter, 7* (4), 4–12.

Mackey, J. A. (1979, June). A history of the Louisiana State University Laboratory School. *National Association of Laboratory Schools Journal,* pp. 59–60.

Mangun, U. L. (1928). *The American normal school.* Baltimore: Warwick and York.

Mayhew, K. C., & Edwards, A. C. (1965). *The Dewey School.* New York: Atheling. (Original work published 1936)

McCarrel, F. (1933). *The development of the training school.* Nashville, TN: George Peabody College for Teachers.

McCaul, R. L. (1961). Dewey and the University of Chicago. *School and Society, 89,* 152–157, 179–183, 202–206.

McCollister, R., Monroe, P., & Tatel, F. (1986). The development of a career ladder model for a laboratory school. *National Association of Laboratory Schools Journal, 11* (1), 27–32.

McConnaughhay, J. W., Jr. (1974). *The status and function of campus laboratory schools in the southeastern United States.* Unpublished doctoral dissertation, Florida State University.

McConnaughhay, J. W., Jr. (1975, February). The status and function of campus laboratory schools in the Southeastern United States. *National Association of Laboratory Schools Newsletter, 15* (4), 8–13.

McGeoch, D. M. (1968). *Function and future: The public campus laboratory schools in Wisconsin.* St. Paul, MN: Upper Midwest Regional Educational Laboratory. (ERIC Document Reproduction Service No. ED 029 814)

McGeoch, D. M. (1971) *The campus laboratory school: Phoenix or dodo bird.* Washington, DC: National Center for Educational Communication (DHEW/OE). (ERIC Document Reproduction Service No. ED 050 046)

McGeoch, D. M. (1972, January). Phoenix or dodo bird? The evolution of the campus laboratory school. *Laboratory School Administrators Association Newsletter, 13* (3), 8–21.

McMurry, F. M., Wood, T. D., Smith, D. E., Farnsworth, C. H., & Richards, G. R. (1904). Theory and practice at Teachers College, Columbia University. In C. A. McMurry (Ed.), *The relation of theory to practice in the education of teachers: The third yearbook of the National Society for the Study of Education* (Part I). Bloomington, IL: Public School Publishing Co.

McPherson, R. B., & McGee, G. W. (1982). Laboratory schools. In H. E. Mitzel (Ed.), *Encyclopedia of educational research* (5th ed., pp. 1019–1022). New York: Macmillan.

Mead, A. R. (1939). Why doesn't the training school make better progress? *Educational Administration and Supervision, 25,* 71–73.

Mead, A. R. (1941). The functions of a laboratory school to its service area. *Educational Administration and Supervision, 27,* 305–308.

Meader, J. L. (1928). *Normal school education in Connecticut* (Contributions to Education, No. 307). New York: Teachers College, Columbia University.

Meriam, J. L. (1906). *Normal school education and efficiency in teaching* (Contributions to Education, No. 1). New York: Teachers College, Columbia University.

Meyer, A. E. (1957). *An educational history of the American people.* New York: McGraw–Hill.

Miller, K. E. (1982, December). *Comparison of inputs in the supervision of laboratory experiences in laboratory school and public school settings.* Paper presented at the meeting of the National Association of Laboratory Schools, Honolulu, HI. (Paper available from author, Burris Laboratory School, Ball State University, Muncie, IN.)

Mitchell, L. S. (1953). *Two lives: The story of Wesley Clair Mitchell and myself.* New York: Simon and Schuster.

Morgan, W. P. (1946). Teachers College laboratory schools. *Phi Delta Kappan, 27,* 167–168.

Myers, R. B. (1970). The role of the laboratory school in curriculum development. In C. R. Blackmon (Ed.), *Laboratory schools,*

U.S.A.—Studies and readings (Southwestern Studies: Humanities Series, No. 3, pp. 128–135). Lafayette: University of Southwestern Louisiana. (ERIC Document Reproduction Service No. ED 045 569)

National Association of Laboratory Schools. (1988). *National Association of Laboratory Schools (NALS) Directory 1988–1989*. Indiana, PA: NALS, Indiana University of Pennsylvania.

National Commission on Teacher Education and Professional Standards. (1962). *Changes in teacher education: Official report of the Columbus conference*. Washington, DC: National Education Association.

National Commission on Teacher Education and Professional Standards. (1969). *A position statement on certification and accreditation*. Washington, DC: National Education Association.

National Education Association. (1887). *Addresses and proceedings*. Washington, DC: the Association.

National Education Association. (1899). Report of the committee on normal schools. *Journal of Proceedings and Addresses*, pp. 836–903.

Nielsen, R. A. (1973, February). Public school aid for laboratory schools. *Laboratory Schools Administrators Association Newsletter, 14*, 20–22.

Norton, A. O. (1926). *The first state normal school in America: The journals of Cyrus Peirce and Mary Swift*. Cambridge, MA: Harvard University Press.

Nudge, M. (1970). Presentation to the governor's commission on educational reform. *Laboratory School Administrators Association Newsletter, 12* (2).

Nuzum, L. H. (1959). *A survey of changes in function of the college-controlled laboratory school from 1948 to 1958.*

Unpublished doctoral dissertation, School of Education, University of Tennessee.

Oestreich, A. (1970). Problems in conducting development in a campus school. *Viewpoints, 46* (2), 47–59.

Office of Education. (1933). *National survey of the education of teachers* (Vols. III & VI). (Bulletin No. 10). Washington, DC: U.S. Government Printing Office.

Ohles, J. F. (1961). The laboratory school: Unresolved problem. *Journal of Teacher Education, 12,* 390–394.

Ohles, J. F. (1967). Is the laboratory school worth saving? *Journal of Teacher Education, 18,* 304–307.

Ohm, R. (Ed.). (1960, January). *Laboratory School Administrators Association Newsletter, 11* (2).

Olson, W. C. (1951). Role of the laboratory school in graduate education. In *Fiftieth Yearbook of the National Society for the Study of Education* (Part I). Chicago: University of Chicago Press.

Otto, H. J. (1947). Comparison of selected organizational and administrative practices in 286 public elementary schools and forty-six campus demonstration schools. *Journal of Educational Research, 41,* 81–87.

Page, F. M., Jr. (1982, Fall). The development of research as a role in laboratory schools. *National Association of Laboratory Schools Journal, 7* (2), 15–19.

Page, J. A. (1983). Laboratory schools: Updated or outdated? *Education, 103,* 372–374.

Page, F. M., Jr., & Page, J. A. (1981). Laboratory schools: Updated or outdated. Statesboro: Georgia Southern College. (ERIC Document Reproduction Service No. ED 213 672)

Pagenkopf, V. E. (1963). *An analysis of professional laboratory experiences provided for prospective teachers in selected teacher education institutions.* Unpublished doctoral dissertation, School of Education, Utah State University.

Painter, W. I. (1962). New media in teacher education. *Phi Delta Kappan, 43,* 389–390.

Pangburn, J. M. (1932). *The evaluation of the American teachers college* (Contributions to Education, No. 500). New York: Teachers College, Columbia University.

Parker, B. G. (1931). *An introductory course in science in the intermediate grades.* Chicago: University of Chicago Press.

Parker, F. R., & Lumpkins, B. (1988). Service roles of laboratory schools as viewed by state department administrators and laboratory school directors. *National Association of Laboratory Schools Journal, 13* (1), 29–33.

Pearson, J. (1970). Where there is no vision, the people perish. *Laboratory School Administrators Association Newsletter, 12* (2).

Perrodin, A. F. (Ed.). (1955). *Functions of laboratory schools in teacher education: Thirty-fourth yearbook.* Lock Haven, PA: Association for Student Teaching.

Perrodin, A. F. (Ed.). (1955a). A symposium—The future of laboratory schools. In A. F. Perrodin (Ed.), *Functions of laboratory schools in teacher education: Thirty-fourth yearbook* (pp. 134–152). Lock Haven, PA: Association for Student Teaching.

Perrodin, A. F. (1955b). The development of laboratory schools in teacher education. In A. F. Perrodin (Ed.), *Functions of laboratory schools in teacher education: Thirty-fourth yearbook* (pp. 1–20). Lock Haven, PA: Association for Student Teaching.

Pulvino, C. J. (1972). The laboratory approach: A vehicle for facilitating American Indian education. *Counseling and Values, 17,* 45–51.

Quick, D. M. (1971). A historical study of the campus laboratory schools in four teacher education institutions in Michigan. *Dissertation Abstracts International, 31*, 3789A–3790A.

Quick, D. M. (1972). Campus laboratory schools: Why are they being eliminated? *Laboratory School Administrators Association Newsletter, 13* (3), 22–30.

Quigley, L. A., & Chaves, A. (Eds.). (1974). *Report of the task force on teacher education and laboratory schools.* Boston: Massachusetts State College System. (ERIC Document Reproduction Service No. ED 131 019)

Rabinowitz, W. (1965, Spring). Changing the laboratory school. *Laboratory School Administrators Association Newsletter, 7* (4), 4–12.

Rabinowitz, W. (1966). Changing the laboratory school. *Harvard Educational Review, 36*, 308–317.

Ramseyer, J. A. (1948). *A study of school improvement with an emphasis upon the role of the laboratory school.* Unpublished doctoral dissertation, College of Education, Ohio State University.

Rasmussen, R. E. (1969). The Wisconsin report on its laboratory schools. *Laboratory School Administrators Association Newsletter, 12* (1), 1–23.

Read, K. (1946). A human relations laboratory. *Journal of Home Economics, 30*, 634–636.

Report to the board of trustees—Ball State University, January 1974. (1974, May). *Laboratory School Administrators Association Newsletter, 15* (2).

Ritter, D. (1976). Process and product of change in the laboratory school function. *National Association of Laboratory Schools Journal, 1* (1).

Roberts, J. C. (1951). *The interrelationship of the training school with the college program of instruction in Western Illinois State College.* Unpublished doctoral dissertation, School of Education, University of Illinois.

The role of the laboratory school in teacher education. (1958). (Proceedings of a conference held at the P. K. Yonge Laboratory School, November 23–25). Gainesville: College of Education, University of Florida.

Rounds, I. (1885). Training of teachers. *Education, 6,* 581–590.

Rucker, W. R. (1952). *A critical analysis of current trends in student teaching.* Unpublished doctoral dissertation, Graduate School of Education, Harvard University.

Rugg, E. U. (1934). Relationships of the laboratory school to the education of teachers. In *American Association of Teachers Colleges Yearbook* (Vol. 13, pp. 78–89). Menasha, WI: G. Banta.

Rugg, H. (1926). Curriculum making in laboratory schools, Chapter V. In *Twenty-sixth yearbook of the National Society for the Study of Education* (Part I, pp. 83–116). Bloomington, IL: Public School Publishing Co.

Rugg, H. (1952). *The teacher of teachers.* New York: Harper and Brothers.

Russell, J. D., & Judd, C. H. (1940). *The American educational system.* Boston: Houghton Mifflin.

Rzepka, L. (1962). The campus school: Its search for identity. *Journal of Teacher Education, 13,* 24–29. (Reprinted in C. R. Blackmon (Ed.), 1970, *Laboratory schools, U.S.A.—Studies and readings* (Southwestern Studies: Humanities Series, No. 3, pp. 36–53). Lafayette: University of Southwestern Louisiana. (ERIC Document Reproduction Service No. ED 045 569))

St. Pierre, R. G. (1979). The role of multiple analyses in quasi-experimental evaluations. *Educational Evaluation and Policy Analysis, 1* (6), 29–35.

Sarason, S. B., Davidson, K. S., & Blatt, B. (1962). *The preparation of teachers: An unstudied problem in education.* New York: John Wiley and Sons.

Saunders, R. W. (1954). *Interrelationships between laboratory schools and other departments of teachers colleges.* Unpublished doctoral dissertation, School of Education, New York University.

Schlichting, H. F. (1953). *The nature and extent of educational research in the laboratory schools of the University of Chicago, 1903–1928.* Unpublished doctoral dissertation, Department of Education, University of Chicago.

Seely, K. R. (1979). Utilization of university facilities for school-age children. *Council of Educational Facility Planners Journal, 17* (6).

Seerley, H. H. (1901). Problems facing the normal school at the opening of the twentieth century. *Education, 21,* 287–290.

Shadick, R. (1966). The interrelationships of the roles of a laboratory school. *Journal of Teacher Education, 17,* 198–204.

Shapiro, A. (1969). The role of the laboratory schools as perceived by the public school administrator. *Midwest Laboratory School Administrators Association, Annual Fall Workshop.* De Kalb: Northern Illinois University. (ERIC Document Reproduction Service No. ED 045 605)

Sherer, L. M., & others. (1961). *The functions and administrative structure of the University Elementary School as a laboratory school of the Department of Education in the School of Education.* Unpublished manuscript, University of California, Los Angeles.

Smith, B. O. (1980). *A design for a school of pedagogy* (Report No. E–80–42000). Washington, DC: U.S. Department of Education.

Smith, B. O. (1983). Closing: Teacher Education in Transition. In D. C. Smith (Ed.), *Essential knowledge for beginning educators* (pp. 140–145). Washington, DC: American Association of Colleges for Teacher Education. (ERIC Document Reproduction Service No. ED 237 455)

Smith, E. D. (1953). *An analysis of the self-evaluation of professional laboratory experience programs in member institutions of the American Association of Colleges for Teacher Education.* Unpublished doctoral dissertation, School of Education, University of Texas.

Smith, E. B., & Johnson, P. (1964). *School-college relationships in teacher education.* Washington, DC: American Association of Colleges for Teacher Education.

Southall, C. T., Jr. (1955). *Laboratory school functions and teacher education.* Unpublished doctoral dissertation, University of Florida.

State University System of Florida. (1969). *Campus laboratory schools in the state university system of Florida.* Tallahassee: Author. (ERIC Document Reproduction Service No. ED 037 419)

Stiles, L. J. (1966, January). *Preparation of teachers and other educational personnel in Hawaii: Study committee report number 1* (A study authorized by the Third Legislature of the State of Hawaii). Honolulu: University of Hawaii.

Stone, M. S. (1923). The first normal school in America. *Teachers College Record, 24,* 263.

Strayer, G. D. (1913). Training of teachers. In P. Monroe (Ed.), *Cyclopedia of Education* (Vol. 5, pp. 515–520). New York: Macmillan.

Stredwick, R. P., & Orlich, D. C. (1973, February). Institutional attitudes towards Northwest Laboratory School programs. *National Association of Laboratory Schools Newsletter, 14,* 22–31.

Stromquist, M. H. (1965). *A study of pre-student teaching laboratory experience in secondary education programs of selected colleges and universities.* Unpublished doctoral dissertation, School of Education, University of Kansas.

Suhrie, A. L. (1930). Standard provisions for equipping and staffing of the laboratory school. *Educational Administration and Supervision, 16,* 345–351.

Surwill, B. (1967). Making a good laboratory school better. *Laboratory School Administrators Association Newsletter, 9* (3).

Tanruther, E. M. (1950). The role of the campus laboratory school in the education of teachers. *Journal of Teacher Education, 1,* 218–223.

Taylor, W. S. (1924). *The development of the professional education of teachers in Pennsylvania.* Philadelphia: Lippincott.

Teachers College. (1946, June). *Report of the special committee of the board of trustees of Teachers College on Horace Mann–Lincoln School.* New York: Columbia University.

Teachers College Record. (1936). *37* (5), 363–447. (Issue devoted to Lincoln School)

Thompson, K. (1964, Spring). Today's image of the laboratory school. *Laboratory School Administrators Association Newsletter, 7* (1), 4–13.

Thompson, M. M. (1938). *An outline of the history of education.* New York: Barnes and Noble.

Thurber, C. M. (1955). The college-controlled laboratory school: Current function. In A. F. Perrodin (Ed.), *Functions of laboratory schools in teacher education: Thirty-fourth yearbook* (pp. 21–31). Lock Haven, PA: Association for Student Teaching.

Traw, L. S. (1979, January). One laboratory school's role in assisting college freshmen making education a career choice. *National Association of Laboratory Schools Journal,* pp. 4–7.

Temble, J. W., Page, F. M., & Page, J. A. (1988). The roles of a teacher education program and laboratory school in preparing pre-service teachers for state assessment. *National Association of Laboratory Schools Journal, 13* (1), 34–42.

Tully, G. E. (1940). A program of studies of a laboratory school. *Educational Administration and Supervision, 26,* 697–700.

Tyler, L. L., & Berchin, A. (Eds.). (1980). Laboratory schools: An unfulfilled potential. *UCLA Educator, 21* (2).

Tyler, R. W. (1980). Why research is needed in education. *UCLA Educator, 21* (2), 4–9.

University High School—1916–1917. *Bulletin of the College of Education of the University of Minnesota, 19* (22), 7–13.

Van Til, W. (1969, February). *The laboratory school: Its rise and fall?* (Address to the national meeting of the Laboratory School Administrators Association, Chicago). Terre Haute: Indiana State University. (ERIC Document Reproduction Service No. ED 034 703)

Van Til, W. (1987). Laboratory schools and the national reports. *National Association of Laboratory Schools Eminent Educator Lecture Series* (Vol. 1, pp. 14–24). Buffalo, NY: National Association of Laboratory Schools.

Venable, T. C. (1960, December). Function of the laboratory school. *Teachers College Journal, 32,* 74–76.

Wagenhorst, L. (1946). The functions of the campus laboratory school of a state teachers college. *Peabody Journal of Education, 23,* 269–273.

Walk, G. E. (1917). Practice teaching and observation in normal schools. *Education, 38,* 69–85.

White, N. D. (1964). *Status and potential of college controlled laboratory schools.* Unpublished doctoral dissertation, George Peabody College for Teachers.

White, N. D. (1965). The status and potential of a representative sample of college-controlled laboratory schools. In P. W. Bixby & H. E. Mitzel (Eds.), *Campus school to a research and dissemination center* (pp. 58–71). University Park: Pennsylvania State

University. (ERIC Document Reproduction Service No. ED 003 774)

Wiles, K. (1958). The role of the laboratory school in educational research. In *The role of the laboratory school in teacher education* (Proceedings of a Conference held at the P. K. Yonge Laboratory School, November 23–25, pp. 19–25). Gainesville: College of Education, University of Florida. (Also in C. R. Blackmon (Ed.), 1970, *Laboratory schools, U.S.A.—Studies and readings* (Southwestern Studies: Humanities Series, No. 3, pp. 115–127). Lafayette: University of Southwestern Louisiana. (ERIC Document Reproduction Service No. ED 045 569)

Williams, E. I. F. (1942). *The actual and potential use of laboratory schools in state normal schools and colleges* (Contributions to Education, No. 846). New York: Teachers College, Columbia University.

Williams, J. (1982, December). *Mission impact of organizational systems within a laboratory school: Leadership roles, organizational structures, and interorganizational relations.* Paper presented at the National Association of Laboratory Schools Research Conference, Honolulu, HI.

Willsey, A. D. (1976, May). The campus school: An educational program in search of direction. *National Association of Laboratory Schools Journal, 2* (1).

Windrow, J. E. (1942). The laboratory school in the teacher education program. *Peabody Journal of Education, 19,* 305–318.

Windrow, J. E. (1948). The function and future of the laboratory school. In *Professional laboratory experiences—An expanding concept in teacher education: Twenty-seventh yearbook* (pp. 83–96). Lock Haven, PA: Association for Student Teaching.

Wirth, A. G. (1964). John Dewey's design for American education: An analysis of aspects of his work at the University of Chicago, 1894–1904. *History of Education Quarterly, 4,* 83–105.

Wolfe, A. M. (1974). *A study of the present and future role of Kentucky college-controlled laboratory schools.* Unpublished doctoral dissertation, Miami University.

Woodring, P. (1960). Future of the teachers college. *Journal of Teacher Education, 11*, 340–342.

Woodruff, A. (1965). Implications for institutional actions. In *The theoretical bases for professional laboratory experiences in teacher education: Forty-fourth yearbook* (pp. 105–113). Cedar Falls, IA: Association for Student Teaching.

Wooten, F. (1969). A study of the value of pre-student teaching experience in a laboratory school. *Illinois School Research, 5* (3), 46–68.

Young, B. J. (1967). *Roles and functions of laboratory schools.* Madison: Wisconsin State University System.

Appendix A

The National Association of Laboratory Schools: A Brief History

Lynn E. Brown, Jr., and Crayton L. Buck

ALTHOUGH NO RECORD EXISTS of professional interaction among laboratory schools before the 1940s, it most certainly occurred from the earliest days of these schools in the mid-1800s. The staffs of laboratory schools, as part of the larger community of teacher educators, certainly took part in the nationwide dialogue. It is known that laboratory school members who attended National Education Association conventions in the 1940s held informal satellite sessions on laboratory school matters. By 1948 the directors of laboratory schools in the north-central states had formed a loose network for exchanging information, comparing understandings, and resolving problems through correspondence. They also met once or twice each year at one another's schools.

In 1956 thirty-four administrators, primarily from the midwest and the far west, attending the conference of the Department of Elementary School Principals (D.E.S.P.), a branch of the National Education Association, met separately to share interests and concerns. They addressed the role of laboratory schools, identified operational policies of concern, and reported on new developments in their schools. The session ended with a consensus favoring further conferences and a more permanent organization.

Robert Fox, of the University of Michigan, invited all laboratory schools to meet in Cincinnati in 1957. Robert Eaves, executive secretary of D.E.S.P., used his office to make the contacts. Fox invited Professor A. Welles Foshay, of Ohio State University, to be the speaker. Foshay, speaking on "Functions and Purposes for Campus Laboratory Schools," stressed the need to redirect laboratory school functions toward experimentation, research, and demonstration, concluding his talk with the following:

> And so I say, in the laboratory schools, we experiment or we perish. I cannot put it more bluntly. We think, or we die. We assert educational leadership, or we leave the parade. A campus school is either a center where educational experimentation is going on, or it has no raison d'etre.

The background was set for a formal organization. Lynn E. Brown, Jr., principal of the Oak Lane Country Day School at Temple University, was given responsibility for organizing a meeting in Philadelphia in 1958 in conjunction with the annual D.E.S.P. conference. The discussion extended and amplified the themes in the Foshay paper. Fox reported on his visits to schools across the country in "A Survey of Laboratory Schools in the United States" in 1958. The conferees developed a series of tentative assumptions about the functions and purposes of campus laboratory schools.

Howd, writing in 1966, recorded the rationale for a professional association:

> Such an organization would (1) increase the contribution of laboratory schools to the improvement of education, (2) promote better communication among laboratory schools, (3) facilitate the consideration of problems confronting laboratory schools, and (4) sponsor such activities as would contribute to the improvement of laboratory school programs. (Howd 1966/1970, 61)

Then the conferees voted to create a formal organization, to be called the Laboratory School Administrators Association (L.S.A.A.).

Its first president was Avard A. Rigby, of Brigham Young University. Andrew D. Rippey, of Fresno State College, joined the slate of officers as vice president; Lynn E. Brown, Jr., became treasurer; and Robert E. Ohm, of the University of Chicago, became newsletter editor. Dr. Fox was asked to draft a constitution and bylaws for action at the next annual meeting.

The group debated the affiliation of the new organization with existing professional bodies. D.E.S.P. continued its support by offering its offices as a home base for the new organization. However, the members opted to hold the annual meetings in conjunction with the American Association of Colleges of Teacher Education (A.A.C.T.E.), recognizing its place in higher education with other affiliated groups, including the Association for Student Teaching, which had a common purpose with laboratory schools. The affiliation with A.A.C.T.E. continues to this day.

At the Chicago convention later in 1958 Margaret Lindsay spoke on "Establishing Evaluative Criteria for Campus Laboratory Schools." The attendees engaged in roundtable discussions related to the address. The adoption of a constitution and bylaws highlighted the meeting.

During the formative years L.S.A.A. was primarily oriented to administrators. School faculty members were very much in the minority, though some made important presentations. Many laboratory school administrators believed that the organization was not meeting its objectives, in part because of this limitation. They changed the bylaws in 1974 to open the membership to all faculty members and to give the organization the more encompassing name National Association of Laboratory Schools.

The infusion of faculty brought vigor and enthusiasm to the organization. The annual convention was lengthened from two to four days to accommodate the large numbers who attended and made presentations. Convention planners set themes and otherwise improved the quality of annual programs. They started a series of invited yearly Eminent Educator addresses. The conventions served to establish linkages and strengthen bonds. Another change in the bylaws encouraged regional meetings, providing additional opportunity for staff members to interact and extend the dialogue among laboratory school people.

Lab school people have been meeting ever since on school campuses in five regions of the country—the west, the midwest, the northeast, the southeast, and the south.

The association grew in size and complexity. In 1978 it created the office of executive secretary to provide a more permanent point of focus to the organization in communication, publication, membership, and support to task forces and committees. Crayton L. Buck became the first executive secretary. Over the past decade the *National Association of Laboratory Schools Journal* was established as a refereed publication, giving members increased opportunity to share their work. Grants from the A. D. Henderson Foundation at Florida Atlantic University have supported the *Journal*. NALS sponsors newsletters, monographs, and task force initiatives. Many, many persons have given time and counsel to the organization and its purposes.

NALS has moved from a tenuous financial position in earlier years to a sound base. The board of directors has established a foundation to supplement dues as a funding source and now makes small grants to faculty to encourage research. The board anticipates larger grants as the foundation's account prospers.

NALS is linking member schools into collaborative ventures. Among the initiatives are conferencing through telecommunications, computer networking, and cooperative development, packaging, and dissemination of curriculum packages. The association enters the final decade of the century in a fine position to help meet the challenges facing education.

Appendix B

Directory of Laboratory Schools

Alabama

EPIC School	University of Alabama	1000 Tenth Avenue, South Birmingham, Alabama 35256
Kilby Laboratory School	University of Northern Alabama	UNA Campus Box 5035, Florence, Alabama 35632
Nursery School	Jacksonville State University	Jacksonville, Alabama 36205
Oakwood Academy	Oakwood College	Huntsville, Alabama 35806
Teaching Learning Center	Jacksonville State University	Jacksonville, Alabama 36265

Arizona

Greyhills High School	Associated with Northern Arizona University	Tuba City, Arizona 86245

Arkansas

Harding Academy	Harding University	Searcy, Arkansas 72143

California

La Sierra Academy	Loma Linda University	Riverside, California 92505

| Seeds University Elementary School | University of California, Los Angeles | 405 Hilgard Avenue, Los Angeles, California 90024 |
| The Farm School | University of California, Irvine | Department of Social Services, Irvine, California 92717 |

Colorado

| Greenlee/Metro Laboratory School | Metropolitan State University | 1150 Lipan Street, Denver, Colorado 80204 |
| UNC Laboratory School | University of Northern Colorado | Greeley, Colorado 80639 |

Connecticut

| Edwin O. Smith School | University of Connecticut | Storrs, Connecticut 06268 |
| School for Young Children | St. Joseph College | West Hartford, Connecticut 06177 |

District of Columbia

| Kendall Demonstration Elementary School | Gallaudet College | 800 Florida Avenue N.E., Washington, D.C. 20002 |
| Model Secondary School for the Deaf | Gallaudet College | 800 Florida Avenue N.E., Washington, D.C. 20002 |

Florida

A. D. Henderson School	Florida Atlantic University	500 N.W. 20th Street, Boca Raton, Florida 33431
Developmental Research School	Florida State University	West Call Street, Tallahassee, Florida 32306
Florida A&M University School	Florida A&M University	P.O. Box A–19, Tallahassee, Florida 32307
Henry S. West Laboratory School	University of Miami	5300 Carillo Street, Coral Gables, Florida 33146

P. K. Yonge Laboratory School	University of Florida	1080 S.W. Eleventh Street, Gainesville, Florida 32611
University School of Nova University	Nova University	7500 S.W. 36th Street, Fort Lauderdale, Florida 33314

Georgia

Berry College Laboratory School	Berry College	P.O. Box 247, Mount Barry Station, Rome, Georgia 30149
Marvin Pittman Laboratory School	Georgia Southern University	Landrum, Box 8004, Statesboro, Georgia 30460

Hawaii

University Laboratory School	University of Hawaii	1776 University Avenue, Honolulu, Hawaii 96822

Illinois

Baker Demonstration School	National College of Education	2840 Sheridan Road, Evanston, Illinois 60201
Laboratory Schools of Illinois State University	Illinois State University	532 DeGarmo Hall, Normal, Illinois 61761
The Laboratory Schools	University of Chicago	1362 East 59th Street, Chicago, Illinois 60637
University High School	University of Illinois	1212 West Springfield Avenue, Urbana, Illinois 61801

Indiana

Burris Laboratory School	Ball State University	Muncie, Indiana 47306
University School	Indiana State University	701 Chestnut Street, Terre Haute, Indiana 47809

Iowa

Malcolm Price Laboratory School	University of Northern Iowa	19th and Campus, Cedar Falls, Iowa 50613

Kansas

| Butcher Children's School | Emporia State University | 1200 Commercial, Emporia, Kansas 66801 |

Kentucky

| Model Laboratory School | Eastern Kentucky University | Richmond, Kentucky 40475 |

Louisiana

A. E. Phillips Laboratory School	Louisiana Tech University	P.O. Box 10168, Tech Station, Ruston, Louisiana 71272
Brown Elementary Laboratory School	Grambling University	Grambling, Louisiana 71245
Grambling Laboratory Middle Magnet School	Grambling University	Grambling, Louisiana 71245
Northwestern State University Laboratory School	Northwestern State University	NSU, Warren Easton Building, Natchitoches, Louisiana 71497
Northwestern State Middle Laboratory School	Northwestern State University	NSU, TEC Building, Natchitoches, Louisiana 71497
Southeastern Louisiana University Laboratory School	Southeastern Louisiana University	P.O. Box 832, University Station, Hammond, Louisiana 70402
Southern University School	Southern University	P.O. Box 9414, Baton Rouge, Louisiana 70813
University Laboratory School	Louisiana State University	Baton Rouge, Louisiana 70803

Maryland

| Lida Lee Tall Learning Resources Center | Towson State University | Towson, Maryland 21204 |

Massachusetts

Eliot–Pearson Children's School	Tufts University	Medford, Massachusetts 02155
Horace Mann Laboratory School	Salem State College	19 Loring Avenue, Salem, Massachusetts 01971
Juniper Park Laboratory School	Westfield State College	Westfield, Massachusetts 01085
Marks Meadow School	University of Massachusetts, Amherst	Amherst, Massachusetts 01003
Martha M. Burnell Laboratory School	Bridgewater State College	Hooper Street, Bridgewater, Massachusetts 02325
McKay Campus School	Fitchburg State College	Fitchburg, Massachusetts 01420
Smith College Campus School	Smith College	Gill Hall, Northampton, Massachusetts 01063

Michigan

Golightly Educational Center	Wayne State University	5536 St. Antoine, Detroit, Michigan 48202
Murdock Elementary School	Andrews University	Berrien Springs, Michigan 49104
University Secondary School	Andrews University	Berrien Springs, Michigan 49104

Minnesota

St. Joseph Laboratory School	College of St. Benedict	Box 488, St. Joseph, Minnesota 56374

Mississippi

Demonstration Elementary School	Mississippi University for Women	MUW Box W1617, Columbus, Mississippi 39701

Missouri

Avila Montessori School	Avila College	Kansas City, Missouri 64145
Greenwood Laboratory School	Southwest Missouri State University	901 South National, Springfield, Missouri 65804
Horace Mann School	Northwest Missouri State University	NWMSU, Brown Hall. Maryville, Missouri 64468
The College School	Webster College	426 Page Avenue, Webster Groves, Missouri 63119

New Hampshire

Wheelock School	Keene State College	24 Adams Street, Keene, New Hampshire 03431

New Jersey

A. Harry Moore Laboratory School	Jersey City College	Jersey City, New Jersey 07305

New York

Bank Street School for Children	Bank Street College	610 West 112th Street, New York, New York 10025
Bishop Dunn Memorial School	Mount St. Mary's College	Gidney Avenue, Newburgh, New York 12550
Campus Learning Center	State University College, Potsdam	Merritt Hall, Potsdam, New York 13676
College Learning Laboratory	Buffalo State College	1300 Elmwood Avenue, Buffalo, New York 14222
Dillon Child Study Center	St. Joseph College	245 Clinton Avenue, Brooklyn, New York 11205
Hunter College Campus Schools	Hunter College	71 East 94th Street, New York, New York 10128

North Carolina

Wahl–Coates Laboratory School	East Carolina State University	East Fifth Street, Greenville, North Carolina 27834

North Dakota

| University Laboratory School | Minot State University | Ninth Avenue N.W., Minot, North Dakota 58701 |

Oklahoma

| Southern Nazarene University School for Children | Southern Nazarene University | 6729 N.W. 39th Expressway, Bethany, Oklahoma 73008 |

Oregon

| Ackerman Laboratory School | Eastern Oregon State College | Eighth and K Streets, La Grande, Oregon 97850 |

Pennsylvania

Carlow College Campus School	Carlow College	3333 5th Avenue, Pittsburgh, Pennsylvania 15213
Centennial School	Lehigh University	815 Pennsylvania Avenue, Bethlehem, Pennsylvania 18018
Children's School	Carnegie Mellon University	MMCC 17, Schenley Park, Pittsburgh, Pennsylvania 15213
Falk School	University of Pittsburgh	Pittsburgh, Pennsylvania 15261
Jenkins Early Childhood Center	Millersville State University	Millersville, Pennsylvania 17551
Miller Research Learning Center	Edinboro University of Pennsylvania	Edinboro, Pennsylvania 16444
Point Park Children's School	Point Park College	Pittsburgh, Pennsylvania 15222
Rowland School for Young Children	Shippensburg State University	Shippensburg, Pennsylvania 17257
School for Exceptional Children	Slippery Rock University	Slippery Rock, Pennsylvania 16057

Temple University Laboratory School	Temple University	Twelfth and Montgomery, Philadelphia, Pennsylvania 19122
University School	Indiana University of Pennsylvania	104 Davis Hall, IUP, Indiana, Pennsylvania 15705
Villa Maria Elementary School	Villa Maria College	819 West Eighth Street, Erie, Pennsylvania 16502

Puerto Rico

Elementary Laboratory School	University of Puerto Rico	Box 23324, UPR Station, San Juan, Puerto Rico 00913

Rhode Island

Henry Barnard School	Rhode Island College	600 Mt. Pleasant Avenue, Providence, Rhode Island 02908

South Carolina

Felton Laboratory School	South Carolina State College	P.O. Box 1537, Orangeburg, South Carolina 29117

Tennessee

Collegedale Academy	Southern Missionary College	Collegedale, Tennessee 37315
Homer Pittard Campus School	Middle Tennessee State University	Box 4, MTSU, Murfreesboro, Tennessee 37132
Memphis State University Campus School	Memphis State University	535 Zach Curlin, Memphis, Tennessee 38152
Spaulding Elementary School	Southern Missionary College	Collegedale, Tennessee 37315
University School	East Tennessee State University	Box 21460–A, ETSU, Johnson City, Tennessee 37614

Texas

Katherine Ryan Child Development Center	Incarnate Word College	4301 Broadway, San Antonio, Texas 78209
School for Young Children	University of St. Thomas	Houston, Texas 77006
St. Martin Hall	Our Lady of the Lake University	411 S.W. 24th Street, San Antonio, Texas 78285

Utah

Edith Bowen Laboratory School	Utah State University	UMC 6700, USU, Logan, Utah 84322

Virginia

Hampton Nongraded Laboratory Schools	Hampton Institute	Hampton, Virginia 23668

Washington

Reid Laboratory School	Eastern Washington University	Cheney, Washington 99004

Wyoming

University School	University of Wyoming	Room 132, Education Building, Laramie, Wyoming 82071

Appendix C

Officers of the National Association of Laboratory Schools

1958

President	Avard A. Rigby, Brigham Young University
Vice president	Andrew Rippey, Fresno State College
Treasurer	Lynn E. Brown, Cortland University
Newsletter editor	Robert Ohm, University of Chicago

1959

President	Andrew Rippey, Fresno State College
Vice president	Philip Lambert, University of Wisconsin
Secretary/treasurer	Marian Brooks, City College of New York
Newsletter editor	Robert Ohm, University of Chicago

1960

President	Philip Lambert, University of Wisconsin
Vice president	Robert Myers, University of Florida
Secretary/treasurer	Helen Johnson, Central Michigan College
Newsletter editor	Alex Frazier, Ohio State University

1961

President	Alex Frazier, Ohio State University
Vice president	David Jackson, University of Illinois
Secretary	Mary Thorp, Rhode Island College
Treasurer	Robert Simpson, Western Washington State College
Newsletter editor	Curtis Howd, Ball State College

1962

President	David Jackson, University of Illinois
Vice president	Curtis Howd, Ball State College
Secretary	Elizabeth Cooper, Virginia State College
Treasurer	William Graham, Florence State College
Newsletter editor	Don Matheson, University of Wisconsin

1963

President	Curtis Howd, Ball State University
Vice president	Roger Brown, University of Illinois
Secretary	Robert Shadrick, Frostburg State College
Treasurer	Willard Jones, University of Wyoming
Newsletter editor	Anthony Schwartz, Plattsburgh State College

1964

President	Roger Brown, University of Illinois
Vice president	Anthony Schwartz, Plattsburgh State College
Secretary	Terrence Snowden, Central Wisconsin College
Treasurer	Robert C. Eicher, University of Wyoming
Newsletter editor	James Carpenter, Western Kentucky State College

1965

President	Anthony Schwartz, Plattsburgh State College
Vice president	James Carpenter, Western Kentucky State College
Corresponding secretary	Curtis Howd, Ball State University
Recording secretary	Leroy Kerns, Northern Colorado College
Newsletter editor	Terrence Snowden, Wisconsin State College

1966

President	James Carpenter, Western Kentucky State College
Vice president	Leroy Kerns, Northern Colorado College
Corresponding secretary	Curtis Howd, Ball State University
Recording secretary	Louis King, Antioch College
Newsletter editor	Terrence Snowden, Wisconsin State College

1967

President	Terrence Snowden, Wisconsin State University
Vice president	Leroy Kerns, Northern Colorado College
Corresponding secretary	Curtis Howd, Ball State University
Recording secretary	Richard Hill, University of Minnesota
Newsletter editor	Don Cholupka, Northern Colorado College

1968

President	Leroy Kerns, Northern Colorado College
Vice president	Harley Lautenschlager, Indiana State University
Corresponding secretary	Curtis Howd, Ball State University
Recording secretary	J. A. Pafford, Georgia Southern College
Newsletter editor	Don Cholupka, Northern Colorado College

1969

President	Harley Lautenschlager, Indiana State University
President-elect	Dick Covington, Central Washington College
Corresponding secretary	Curtis Howd, Ball State University
Recording secretary	Ross Nielsen, University of Northern Iowa
Newsletter editor	C. Robert Blackmon, University of Southwestern Louisiana

1970

President	Dick Covington, Central Washington College
Vice president	Ross Nielsen, University of Northern Iowa
Corresponding secretary	Jerry Duea, University of Northern Iowa
Newsletter editor	Art Brill, Emporia State College

1971

President	Ross Nielsen, University of Northern Iowa
President-elect	Anthony Gregorec, Northern Illinois University
Corresponding secretary	Jerry Duea, University of Northern Iowa
Recording secretary	Terrence Boylan, Rhode Island College
Newsletter editor	George A. Gogo, Northern Illinois University

1972

President	Anthony Gregorec, Northern Illinois University
President-elect	John C. Pearson, University of Wisconsin, Stevens Point
Corresponding secretary	Jerry Duea, University of Northern Iowa
Recording secretary	Sister Arlene Hugulet, Alverno College
Newsletter editor	George A. Gogo, Northern Illinois University

1973

President	John C. Pearson, University of Wisconsin, Stevens Point
President-elect	Edward J. Bass, Florida State University
Corresponding secretary	Jerry Duea, University of Northern Iowa
Recording secretary	Juanita Park
Newsletter editor	Kenneth Frisbie, University of Northern Colorado

1974

President	Edward J. Bass, Florida State University
President-elect	Robert Hymer, University of Wyoming
Corresponding secretary	Jerry Duea, University of Northern Iowa
Recording secretary	Charles Snethen, University of Missouri
Newsletter editor	Kenneth Frisbie, University of Northern Colorado

1975

President	Robert Hymer, University of Wyoming
President-elect	Robert Hearn, Louisiana Tech University
Corresponding secretary	Jerry Duea, University of Northern Iowa
Recording secretary	Charles Snethen, University of Missouri
Newsletter editor	Kenneth Frisbie, University of Northern Colorado

1976

President	Robert Hearn, Louisiana Tech University
President-elect	Raymond Schmelter, University of Wisconsin, Oshkosh
Corresponding secretary	Edward Vertuno, Florida State University
Recording secretary	Charles Snethen, University of Missouri
Journal editor	Kenneth Frisbie, University of Northern Colorado

1977

President	Raymond Schmelter, University of Wisconsin, Oshkosh
President-elect	Crayton L. Buck, Longwood College
Corresponding secretary	Edward Vertuno, Florida State University
Recording secretary	Charles Snethen, University of Missouri
Journal editor	Kenneth Frisbie, University of Northern Colorado

1978

President	Crayton L. Buck, Longwood College
President-elect	James Jester, Southwest Missouri State University
Corresponding secretary	Edward Vertuno, Florida State University
Recording secretary	Charles Branch, Ball State University
Journal editor	Kenneth Frisbie, University of Northern Colorado

1979

President	James Jester, Southwest Missouri State University
President-elect	Kenneth Frisbie, University of Northern Colorado
Corresponding secretary	Crayton L. Buck, Longwood College
Recording secretary	Roger Spugnardi, Potsdam State College
Journal editor	Kenneth Frisbie, University of Northern Colorado

1980

President	Kenneth Frisbie, University of Northern Colorado
President-elect	Richard Sevey, Rhode Island College
Executive secretary	Crayton L. Buck, Longwood College
Recording secretary	Barbara Pass, James Madison University
Journal editor	Robert Hymer, University of Wyoming

1981

President	Richard Sevey, Rhode Island College
President-elect	Loretta Krause, University of Hawaii
Executive secretary	Crayton L. Buck, Longwood College
Recording secretary	Barbara Pass, James Madison University
Journal editor	Robert Hymer, University of Wyoming

1982

President	Loretta Krause, University of Hawaii
President-elect	Warner Tobin, Indiana University of Pennsylvania
Executive secretary	Crayton L. Buck, Longwood College
Recording secretary	Lynn McCarthy, National College of Education
Journal editor	Robert Hymer, University of Wyoming

1983

President	Warner Tobin, Indiana University of Pennsylvania
President-elect	Gene McDonald, Southeast Louisiana State University
Executive secretary	Crayton L. Buck, Manassas Park School Division, Virginia
Recording secretary	Lynn McCarthy, National College of Education
Journal editor	Robert Hymer, Jacksonville State University

1984

President	Gene McDonald, Southeast Louisiana State University
President-elect	Lynn McCarthy, National College of Education
Executive secretary	Crayton L. Buck, Manassas Park School Division, Virginia
Recording secretary	Barbara Bittner, Florida Atlantic University
Journal editor	Robert Hymer, Jacksonville State University

1985

President	Lynn McCarthy, National College of Education
President-elect	Kenneth Miller, Ball State University
Executive secretary	Crayton L. Buck, State University College, Buffalo
Recording secretary	Barbara Bittner, Florida Atlantic University
Journal editor	Robert Hymer, Jacksonville State University

1986

President	Kenneth Miller, Ball State University
President-elect	Barbara Bittner, Florida Atlantic University
Executive secretary	Crayton L. Buck, State University College, Buffalo
Recording secretary	Jackson J. Martin, Eastern Washington University
Journal editor	Robert Hymer, Jacksonville State University

1987

President	Barbara Bittner, Florida Atlantic University
President-elect	Alvin Fabre, Louisiana State University
Executive secretary	Crayton L. Buck, State University College, Buffalo
Deputy exec. secretary	John R. Johnson, Indiana University of Pennsylvania
Recording secretary	Jackson J. Martin, University of Wyoming
Journal editor	Robert Hymer, Jacksonville State University

1988

President	Alvin Fabre, Louisiana State University
President-elect	Gregory R. Ulm, Indiana State University
Executive secretary	John R. Johnson, Indiana University of Pennsylvania
Deputy exec. secretary	Crayton L. Buck, State University College, Buffalo
Recording secretary	James Fox, Louisiana State University
Journal editor	Robert Hymer, Jacksonville State University

1989

President	Gregory R. Ulm, Indiana State University
President-elect	Mina Bayne, University of Wyoming
Executive secretary	John R. Johnson, Indiana University of Pennsylvania
Recording secretary	James Fox, Louisiana State University
Journal editor	Robert Hymer, Jacksonville State University

1990

President	Mina Bayne, University of Wyoming
President-elect	James Fox, Louisiana State University
Executive secretary	John R. Johnson, Indiana University of Pennsylvania
Recording secretary	Sandra Tsurutome, Florida Atlantic University
Journal editor	Robert Hymer, Jacksonville State University

1991

President	James Fox, Louisiana State University
President-elect	Judith Hechtman, Indiana University of Pennsylvania
Executive secretary	John R. Johnson, Indiana University of Pennsylvania
Recording secretary	Gregory R. Ulm, Indiana State University
Journal editor	Robert Hymer, Jacksonville State University

Appendix D

NALS Distinguished Service Awards

BEGINNING IN 1979, the National Association of Laboratory School has annually honored a person who performed exemplary service for the association. These are the people who have been so honored.

Crayton L. Buck	Longwood College	1979
Kenneth Frisbie	University of Northern Colorado	1980
Lynn E. Brown	Cortland University	1981
Robert Hymer	Jacksonville State University	1982
Ross Nielsen	University of Northern Iowa	1983
James Jester	Southwest Missouri State University	1984
Loretta Krause	University of Hawaii	1985
Richard Sevey	Rhode Island College	1986
Gene McDonald	Southeast Louisiana State University	1987
Warner Tobin	Indiana University of Pennsylvania	1987

Kenneth Miller	Ball State University	1988
Ann Baldwin Taylor	Carnegie Mellon University	1989
Barbara Bittner	Florida Atlantic University	1990
Alvin Fabre	Louisiana State University	1991

Appendix E

NALS Benefactors

Gold Patrons

Lynn E. Brown   Cortland, New York

Takayoshi Mizushima   The Cultural Foundation for Promoting the National Costume of Japan, Tokyo, Japan

Masanori Sugo   Nishinippon Junior College High School, Yame, Japan

In honor of Loretta Krause

Kazumasa Okuda   Director, Sohseikan High School, Isahaya, Japan

Silver Patrons

Baker Demonstration School	National College of Education
Barbara Bittner	Florida Atlantic University
Crayton L. Buck	State University College, Buffalo
Judith Hechtman	Indiana University of Pennsylvania
Robert Hymer	Jacksonville State University
Loretta Krause	University of Hawaii
Gene McDonald	Southeast Louisiana State University
Ross Nielsen	University of Northern Iowa
Price Laboratory School	University of Northern Iowa
Jean Sakihara	University of Hawaii
Richard Sevey	Rhode Island College
Ann Baldwin Taylor	Carnegie Mellon University
Warner Tobin	Indiana University of Pennsylvania
Sandra Tsurutome	Florida Atlantic University

Frances Tyau   State University College, Buffalo
Gregory R. Ulm   Indiana State University School

Sustaining Patrons

Norish Adams   Florida A&M University
Sarah Anderson   State University College, Buffalo
Mary Gullickson   University of Hawaii
James Hantula   University of Northern Iowa
James Jester   Southwest Missouri State University
Rita King   Middle Tennessee State University
Rowland Laboratory School   Shippensburg State University
College Learning Laboratory   Speech/Language Department
                                    In honor of Crayton L. Buck
Mississippi University for Women   In memory of Cille Crowe

Donors

Kathryn Aschlimann   Goshen College
Carolee Kramer   Ball State University
Warren Royer   University of Illinois
Anthony Schwartz   State University College, Plattsburgh